THE
WICKED WIT
OF THE
ROYAL
FAMILY

Also by Karen Dolby

The Wicked Wit of Queen Elizabeth II
The Wicked Wit of Prince Philip
The Wicked Wit of Princess Margaret

THE
WICKED WIT
↝ OF THE ↜
ROYAL
FAMILY

Compiled by Karen Dolby

Michael O'Mara Books Limited

First published in Great Britain in 2019 by
Michael O'Mara Books Limited
9 Lion Yard
Tremadoc Road
London SW4 7NQ

A CIP catalogue record for this book is available from the
British Library.

Papers used by Michael O'Mara Books Limited are natural,
recyclable products made from wood grown in sustainable forests.
The manufacturing processes conform to the environmental
regulations of the country of origin.

ISBN: 978-1-78929-179-7 in hardback print format
ISBN: 978-1-78929-180-3 in ebook format

1 2 3 4 5 6 7 8 9 10

Designed and typeset by K.DESIGN, Winscombe, Somerset
Printed and bound by CPI Group (UK) Ltd, Croydon CR0 4YY

www.mombooks.com

Contents

Introduction

'With the Royal Family, you don't want to see them as people because it takes the sheen off. They're distant; you can idealize them. But there's room to have compassion for people and see them as human beings. Just because they're royalty, it doesn't mean they don't love or feel loss or feel pain.'

CLAIRE FOY, WHO PLAYED THE YOUNG QUEEN ELIZABETH IN *The Crown*

They may be royal, their day-to-day lives may be governed by tradition and protocol, the dignity that comes with duty, but in many ways the Royal Family are just like us, especially in their dealings with one another.

Whatever the stresses and strains, this is a family who laugh together, who joke, and who are happy to tease and be teased. Recent photos often show them laughing uproariously and sharing private asides.

Press and public alike have long been fascinated by Prince Philip's sense of humour and notorious gaffes. Even more of his hilarious comments and witty one-liners are reserved for his wife and family in private. Prince Harry once said of his grandparents: 'They are very funny together. My family is the same as any other family when it comes to humour behind closed doors.'

The Queen, too, is known to have a wickedly dry sense of humour. The former Archbishop of Canterbury, Dr Rowan Williams, came to know Her Majesty well and commented, 'I have found in the Queen someone who can be friendly, who can be informal, who can be extremely funny in private – and not everybody appreciates how funny she can be.'

The younger generation of royals seem to take a joyful approach to duty and are often seen smiling and joking. Their genuine affection and ease with their partners and family is apparent. Prince Harry in particular is known for his sense of fun and is said to have once recorded a message on his grandmother's mobile phone, so that anyone calling the Queen was greeted by 'Hey, wassup? This is Liz.' And Prince William revealed that it was humour that originally drew him to Kate, confessing, 'She's got a really naughty sense of humour, which really helps me because I've got a really dry sense of humour so it was good fun …'

Over the years, members of the Royal Family have found a way of reconciling their very public images with their private personas. This book looks at the real personalities behind the images and the humour that underlies their dealings with each other, and touches on every aspect of their lives. From quick-witted retorts to clever comments and wise words, the wicked wit of the Royal Family can be found in stories and anecdotes, and in their own unedited speeches as they enjoy the lighter side of life.

CHAPTER 1

A Royal Guide
to Romance

When it comes to royal romance, the gold standard has to be the Queen and Prince Philip. Married for over seventy years, the Queen described her husband on their golden wedding anniversary in 1997: 'He has, quite simply, been my strength and stay all these years.' Until his retirement from official duties in autumn 2017, Philip had stood beside his wife at every major event and accompanied her on royal visits worldwide. Like any married couple, their relationship may not always have been plain sailing and there have been some bumps along the way, but there is no doubting their obviously genuine affection, respect and delight in one another's company. You only have to see them laughing together or sharing a private comment to know that here is a couple in harmony.

Young Love

Elizabeth and Philip were first briefly introduced at a family wedding in 1934 when she was just eight years old. Five years later, when Elizabeth was thirteen and Philip an eighteen-year-old naval cadet, they met again at the Royal Naval College in Dartmouth. Philip was asked to look after princesses Elizabeth and Margaret who were visiting with the King and Queen. Philip was dashing, dynamic and athletic, played tennis and made Elizabeth laugh. The young Princess was smitten and later the two began exchanging letters. At some point during the war years, Elizabeth started to keep a photograph of her future husband on her bedside table.

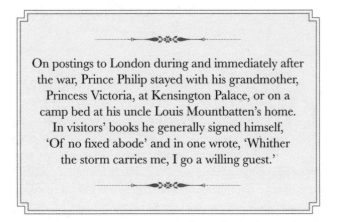

On postings to London during and immediately after
the war, Prince Philip stayed with his grandmother,
Princess Victoria, at Kensington Palace, or on a
camp bed at his uncle Louis Mountbatten's home.
In visitors' books he generally signed himself,
'Of no fixed abode' and in one wrote, 'Whither
the storm carries me, I go a willing guest.'

In June 1946, Philip wrote to Elizabeth apologizing for having
invited himself to Buckingham Palace. He thought he had
a 'monumental cheek ... Yet however contrite I feel, there
is always a small voice that keeps saying "nothing ventured,
nothing gained" – well did I venture and I gained a wonderful
time.'

Elizabeth and Philip were married at Westminster Abbey on
20 November 1947. Two thousand guests were invited to the
ceremony, which was recorded and broadcast by BBC Radio
to 200 million people around the world. Elizabeth's dress was
designed by Norman Hartnell and, due to wartime rationing
measures still in place, was paid for with clothing ration coupons.

Winston Churchill described the wedding as 'a flash of
colour on the hard road we have to travel' while Queen Mary's
lady-in-waiting wrote, 'A week of gaiety such as the court has not
seen for years. There were parties in St James's Palace to view
the wedding presents, a royal dinner party for all the foreign
royalties, and an evening party at Buckingham Palace which
seemed after the years of austerity like a scene out of a fairytale.'

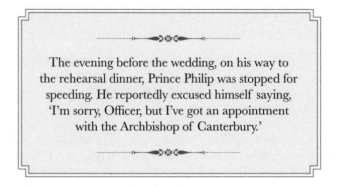

> The evening before the wedding, on his way to the rehearsal dinner, Prince Philip was stopped for speeding. He reportedly excused himself saying, 'I'm sorry, Officer, but I've got an appointment with the Archbishop of Canterbury.'

Just 150 guests were invited to the wedding breakfast, a sign of the austerity in Britain in the post-war years. Elizabeth and Philip spent their wedding night at Broadlands, the Mountbatten family estate in Hampshire, travelling there by train with the Princess's corgi, Susan. Their real honeymoon was in snowbound Birkhall on the Balmoral estate.

As a surprise present for their sixtieth wedding anniversary in 2007, Philip took the Queen back to Broadlands and then to Malta, the island where they lived as a young married couple when Philip was stationed there by the Royal Navy between 1949 and 1951.

♛

Speaking on ITV's *Our Queen at Ninety* documentary in 2016, the Duchess of Cambridge commented on the strength of the Queen and Prince Philip's relationship: 'All the time, William and I are so struck by the Queen's sense of duty and commitment. And I think to do that by yourself would be a very lonely place to be. But I think to have the support of your husband there by your side on those occasions – and behind closed doors as well – I think is really special.' She added, 'William and I have got quite a long way to go, but no, it really, really is fantastic.'

Royal Rumours

As a teenager during World War II, the media had other concerns when the Queen was growing up. The first hints of a romance between her and Prince Philip came after the wedding of Patricia Mountbatten to Lord Brabourne in October 1946. The Princess and the Prince were captured on film gazing at one another, framed by the doorway of Romsey Abbey, but rumours were unconfirmed. Other royals did not get off so lightly.

One of the first to feel the full glare of the media spotlight was Princess Margaret. With her sister married in 1947, attention turned to the younger royal. An American headline of the time said, 'She is Britain's Number One item for public scrutiny,' going on to announce, 'People are more interested in her than in the House of Commons or the dollar crisis.' She was also dubbed the 'party princess' and, later, the 'tragic princess' who loved and lost, after she renounced her intention of marrying divorcee Group Captain Peter Townsend.

The merest whiff of a royal romance is enough to send the media rumour mill into a frenzy, whether or not there is any truth in the speculation. As the young heir to the throne, Prince Charles in his twenties was considered one of the world's most eligible bachelors. He was seen as something of a daredevil – parachuting, surfing, playing polo and riding to hunt – and was quickly nicknamed 'Action Man'.

The press constantly linked him to beautiful young women and Charles once complained, 'I've only got to look twice at someone and the next morning I'm engaged to her.'

In March 1975, he said, 'I have read so many reports recently telling everyone who I am about to marry that when last year a certain young lady was staying at Sandringham a crowd of about ten thousand appeared when we went to church. Such was the obvious conviction that what they had read was true that I almost felt I had better espouse myself at once so as not to disappoint too many people.' He was probably speaking about American Laura Watkins who, as a Catholic, was barred from marrying the heir to the throne.

> When touring India in 1981, a well-known film actress asked if she could kiss Prince Charles. 'Why not?' he replied. 'Everyone else does.'

Charles was aware that not everyone's interest was genuine and said, 'Various professional ladies hurl themselves without warning against one's person while one is emerging innocently from boiling surf or having executed a turn on a ski slope. All this may be harmless publicity and good for the ladies' careers, but what do you think it does to my ego?'

He obviously knew that the press had an unending interest in such images: 'All the newspapers seem to be interested in are pictures of me falling off a horse or having a girl fling her arms round my neck. You'd think it was the only thing I ever did.'

Labelled 'Prince Charming' by the Canadian press, it's fair to say that the young Prince Andrew had a racy reputation. The relationship that really sealed his image in the public eye was with the American model, actress and photographer Koo Stark in 1982.

When the Queen saw the headlines apparently her only comment was, 'Why don't they call you by your real names, Andrew and Katherine?' When asked about his nicknames Andrew said, 'Goodness. No comment. That's too dangerous.' And on the subject of girlfriends: 'Girls? I like them as much as the next guy.'

When Prince Edward was a student at Cambridge University, he commented ruefully, 'I have a whole lot of friends at Cambridge, but you can't be exclusive, it's as simple as that. The media can make what they like of anything. You only have to be seen in the company of one person more than three times and you are instantly virtually married to them.'

Princess Diana had a similar experience, after her separation from Charles. 'Any gentleman that's been past my door, we've instantly been put together in the media and all hell's broken loose, so that's been very tough on the male friends I've had and obviously from my point of view.'

Prince William also found the constant scrutiny intense. 'There's been a lot of speculation about every single girl I'm with and it actually does quite irritate me after a while, more so because it's a complete pain for the girls.'

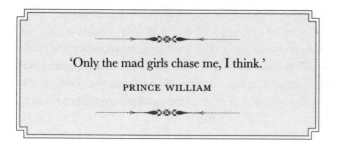

'Only the mad girls chase me, I think.'

PRINCE WILLIAM

'Whatever "In Love" Means'

Ignoring the many rumoured romances, Charles's genuine relationships were always discreet. There were quite a few, and every time a name was added to the list the media would go into overdrive assessing every aspect of the new girlfriend and her potential as a future royal bride.

Questioned about his views on marriage, as he often was, Charles said, 'I'd want to marry someone whose interests I could share. A woman not only marries a man, she marries into a way of life – a job. If I'm deciding on whom I want to live with for fifty years – well, that's the last decision on which I would want my head to be ruled by my heart.'

Interviewed shortly after their engagement in 1981, Charles and Diana were asked if they were in love. Diana answered instantly 'Of course' while Charles replied, 'Whatever "in love" means.' Years later, after their separation, Diana said in an interview, 'That threw me completely. I thought what a strange question and answer. God. Absolutely traumatized me.'

Their wedding took place on 29 July 1981 at St Paul's Cathedral. It's estimated that 750 million people watched world-wide, and at the time it was described as a 'fairytale' and the 'wedding of the century'. During the ceremony, Diana repeated the names of her husband-to-be in the wrong order – 'Philip Charles Arthur George' – prompting Prince Andrew to joke, 'She's married my father!'

Charles also confused his vows leaving out 'worldly' and promising instead to share all Diana's goods with her, at which point Princess Anne quipped, '*That* was no mistake!'

Just two weeks into their marriage, when Charles and Diana came to stay at Balmoral after their honeymoon cruise on board *Britannia*, the cracks in their relationship were already showing. Diana was moody and withdrawn, very different from the happy, easy-going young woman she had seemed.

Prince Philip found their stay difficult, saying of Diana, 'It was just impossible. She didn't appear for breakfast. At lunch she sat with her headphones on, listening to music, and then she would disappear for a walk or run.'

Diana loved her Walkman explaining, 'I'm a great believer in having music wherever I go. And it's just a big treat to go out for a walk with music still coming with me.' The Queen had a different take: 'She can't hear anybody coming with that contraption, you know. She just walks straight past me.' And, she added, 'She's like a nervy racehorse. She needs careful handling.'

As far as Diana was concerned, 'I like to be a free spirit. Some don't like that, but that's just the way I am.'

Andrew and Sarah

When asked what his ideal partner would be like, Prince Andrew was frank: 'The honest answer is that I don't know what I'm looking for yet, simply because I haven't had any chance to think about it.' Furthermore, 'I know that if I do find somebody then it is going to come like a lightning bolt, and you're going to know it there and then.'

Andrew and Sarah Ferguson first met as children, but did not become romantically involved until 1985 when they met again at a party. The Queen thought Fergie would make an ideal partner for her lively second son: 'He's met his match this time!'

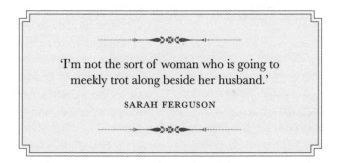

'I'm not the sort of woman who is going to meekly trot along beside her husband.'

SARAH FERGUSON

They were married on 23 July 1986 at Westminster Abbey. Sarah said at the time, 'I married Her Majesty the Queen's best-looking son.' She also declared, 'He loves the madness of me.'

All in the Timing

Prince Edward met Sophie Rhys-Jones through work in 1994. Their engagement was announced in January 1999, and they married at St George's Chapel Windsor in June that year.

Interviewed at the time, Edward explained, 'It's impossible for anybody else to understand why it has taken me so long. But I don't think it had been right before and I don't think Sophie would have said yes. Hopefully the fact that she has said yes means I've got the timing right.' Asked about the possibility of children he said reasonably enough, 'Let's take one step at a time.'

Charles and Camilla

Prince Charles met the young Camilla Shand long before Lady Diana Spencer. At the time Camilla's lineage was not considered noble enough for marriage to the heir to the throne. Charles followed tradition and ignored his heart, and Camilla married Andrew Parker-Bowles in 1973 (they divorced in 1995). It is said that Charles and Camilla reconnected in the months following the traumatic murder in 1979 of the Prince's beloved uncle and mentor, Lord Louis Mountbatten, and their affair apparently resumed around 1986 when Charles's relationship with Diana had already become toxic.

When the couple first met in 1970, Camilla is reported to have joked to Charles, 'My great-grandmother was your great-great-grandfather's mistress, so how about it?' (Her maternal great-grandmother was Alice Keppel, King Edward VII's long-time mistress from 1898 to 1910.) 'It' later led to tying the knot, and after the announcement of their engagement in February

2005 Camilla said, 'I'm just coming down to earth.' Charles added, 'Just a couple of middle-aged people getting wed.'

The Queen and Prince Philip were not present at Charles's and Camilla's civil wedding on 9 April 2005 at the Guildhall in Windsor, prompting some speculation that this reflected her feelings about the marriage. It was actually a reflection of the Queen's constitutional position and traditional faith, and not a sign of disapproval. Her genuine happiness at the occasion was apparent in her warm speech later that day.

She began by joking that she had an important announcement about the Grand National winner, and continued that Charles and Camilla 'have overcome Becher's Brook and The Chair [the highest fences in the race] and all kinds of other obstacles. They have come through and I'm very proud and wish them well. My son is home and dry with the woman he loves. Welcome to the winner's enclosure.'

When asked about his father's remarriage, Harry said, 'She's a wonderful woman, and she's made our father very, very happy, which is the most important thing. William and I love her to bits. She's not the wicked stepmother.'

After meeting her future stepsons for the first time in 1998, Camilla admitted, 'I really need a gin and tonic.'

The Next Generation

A university friend told Kate how lucky she was to be dating Prince William when they were both students at St Andrew's. Smiling, Kate quickly responded, 'He's lucky to have me.'

Looking back to when they were first introduced, Kate recalled, 'Well, I actually think I went bright red when I met you and sort of scuttled off, feeling very shy about meeting you.' William added, 'When I first met Kate I knew there was something very special about her. I knew there was possibly something that I wanted to explore there. We ended up being friends for a while and that just sort of was a good foundation. Because I do generally believe now that being friends with one another is a massive advantage. And it just went from there.'

Increasingly in the media spotlight and under press pressure, William and Kate called it quits in April 2007. William apparently said at the time, 'I can't. It just isn't going to work … it isn't fair to you.'

Before their break-up became official, rumours flew when William was spotted dancing with models at a nightclub, ending the evening by leaping onto a table yelling, 'I'm free!' After a holiday with her mother in Ireland, Kate threw herself into training with an all-female rowing team called Sisterhood, and also partied hard. But the break didn't last long and by June that year the couple were back together.

Years later, Kate said of that period, 'At the time I wasn't very happy about it, but it actually made me a stronger person. You find out things about yourself that maybe you hadn't realized. I think you can get quite consumed by a relationship when you are younger, and I really valued that time for me as well, although I didn't think it at the time.'

Talking about each other, William claimed, 'Obviously we both have a very fun time together, both have a very good sense of humour about things, we're down to earth, we take the mickey out of each other a lot, and she's got plenty of habits that make me laugh that I tease her about.'

The Prince also brought up the rumour that Kate had a picture of him on her wall when boarding at Marlborough College. William joked, 'There wasn't just one, there were about twenty.' Kate laughed, 'He wishes. No, I had the Levi's guy on my wall, not a picture of William, sorry.' 'It was me in Levi's obviously,' William quipped.

William and Kate announced their engagement in November 2010 and both their families were delighted. Prince Charles commented, 'They've been practising for long enough,' while Camilla was more effusive, 'It's the most brilliant news. I'm just so happy and so are they. It's wicked.'

Asked why he had waited so long, William grinned: 'I don't remember how many years it's been. I also didn't realize it was a race, otherwise I would have been a lot quicker.' More seriously, he added, 'I wanted to give her a chance to see in and to back out if she needed to before it all got too much. I'm trying to learn from lessons in the past, and I just wanted to give her the best chance to settle and to see what happens on the other side.'

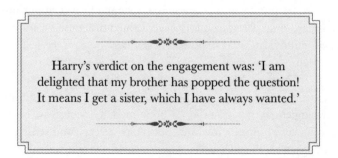

Harry's verdict on the engagement was: 'I am delighted that my brother has popped the question! It means I get a sister, which I have always wanted.'

William also revealed, 'I was torn between asking Kate's dad first and then the realization that he might actually say no dawned upon me. So I thought if I ask Kate first then he can't really say no.' And, 'I'd been planning it for a while but as any guy out there will know it takes a certain amount of motivation to get yourself going.'

When asked how they were both feeling, William said, 'We're like sort of ducks, very calm on the surface with little feet going under the water.'

Prince William proposed to Kate in the autumn of 2010. The setting was romantic: a secluded log cabin in the foothills of Mount Kenya. He said later, 'I didn't really plan it that far in advance. I just knew I wanted it to feel comfortable where I did it.' He also commented, 'You hear a lot of horror stories about proposing and things going horribly wrong – it went really, really well and I was really pleased when she said yes.'

He proposed with his mother's sapphire ring, 'I had been carrying it around with me in my rucksack for about three weeks before that and I literally would not let it go. Everywhere I went I was keeping hold of it because I knew this thing, if it disappeared, I would be in a lot of trouble.'

He explained the heartfelt significance of giving Kate Diana's ring: 'It's my mother's engagement ring so I thought it was quite nice because obviously she's not going to be around to share any of the fun and excitement of it all – this was my way of keeping her close to it all.' He added, 'It's very special to me. As Kate's very special to me now, it was right to put the two together.'

And what of Prince Harry and Meghan Markle? Harry said it all: 'This beautiful woman just literally tripped and fell into my life.' And, he added, 'I was beautifully surprised when I walked into that room and saw her. I thought, I'm really gonna have to up my game, sit down and make sure I have a good chat. She's capable of anything.'

Early in their relationship, in an interview with *Vanity Fair* magazine, Meghan spoke about trying to guard their privacy. 'This is for us. It's part of what makes it so special, that it's just ours.' And 'just ours' got public confirmation in November 2016. Yes, Harry really was in a relationship with the American actress, and they made their first official public appearance together at the Invictus Games in Toronto that year.

When Clarence House and Kensington Palace announced their engagement on 27 November 2017, the media and public had a new obsession. 'When did I know she was "The One"?' Harry's answer was simple. 'The very first time we met.'

Meghan added, 'We're two people who are really happy and in love.' And speaking of Harry's proposal, 'It was just an amazing surprise. It was so sweet and natural and very romantic … I could barely let him finish proposing, like, "Can I say yes now?!"'

Shortly before their wedding Harry stated, 'I knew that at the end of the day, she chooses me. I choose her. Whatever we have to tackle will be us together as a team.'

Their wedding took place on 19 May 2018 at St George's Chapel, Windsor Castle. Royal watchers collectively sighed when Harry was seen turning to greet his bride at the altar: 'You look amazing.' And later, referring to Princess Diana, he added, 'If my mother was here now, she and Meghan would be as thick as thieves.'

Mr and Mrs

When the Queen and Prince Philip had been married for fifty years in 1997, Philip was asked for his advice on what made a successful marriage. 'Tolerance is the one essential ingredient … You can take it from me that the Queen has the quality of tolerance in abundance.' But what about him? Patient? Moody?

In 1994, on the deck of *Britannia*, keen to set sail from Belize, Philip leaned over the rail and shouted to his wife, 'Yak, yak, yak. Come on, get a move on!' The Queen was still chatting to their hosts on the quayside. And on another occasion, again on the royal yacht, the Queen is reported to have announced, 'I'm not coming out of my cabin until he's in a better temper. I'm going to stay here on my bed until he's better.'

But he knows when to crack a joke. Crossing to Vancouver Island, on a visit to Canada, stormy weather rocked the yacht just as a young officer attempted to serve afternoon tea. The tray of cakes crashed to the floor, whereupon Philip helped pick them up. Sitting back down next to his wife he joked, 'I've got mine. Yours are down there.'

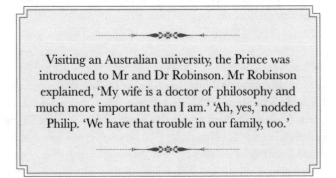

Visiting an Australian university, the Prince was introduced to Mr and Dr Robinson. Mr Robinson explained, 'My wife is a doctor of philosophy and much more important than I am.' 'Ah, yes,' nodded Philip. 'We have that trouble in our family, too.'

On the subject of husbands and wives and cars, he once quipped, 'When a man opens a car door for his wife, it's either a new car or a new wife.' And when Philip commissioned an open-top Aston Martin for himself in 1954, he had it fitted with a telephone from which he would make spoof calls to his wife, disguising his voice. He also asked for an extra rear-view mirror in order that 'My wife can adjust her hat', or so he said.

And the Queen … At a lunch at the British Embassy in Moscow during her 1994 state visit, she was sitting beside the embassy doctor, Hugh Carpenter. He was talking so animatedly to Her Majesty that his wife began gesticulating at him from across the room as if to say, 'Stop talking so much!' The Queen noticed and found this very funny, saying, 'I must try that on Philip some time.'

Heard the one about the whale? When Diana pointed to a 'Save the Whales' poster she joked to Charles, 'Look, darling, they're trying to save us', but he was not amused. She commented, 'He never laughs at my jokes.' Or the vampire joke? Charles presented Camilla with an unusual present, calling, 'Darling, darling, come and see what I have got for you.' It was a necklace designed to protect the wearer from vampire bites.

Can you imagine William and Kate on *Masterchef*? Kate confessed to being a terrible cook at a gala dinner in 2016. 'Kate's cooking is the reason I'm so skinny,' was William's speedy verdict on his wife's skills. But, he also added, when they were first dating he used to try and showcase his own culinary talent. 'When I was trying to impress Kate I was trying to cook these amazing fancy dinners and … I would burn something, something would overspill, something would catch fire and she would be sitting in the background just trying to help, and basically taking control of the whole situation.'

William the Bald. When asked why the couple were late arriving at a function, Kate jokingly replied, 'William had to do his hair.' And once, at the end of a shearing demonstration, she was handed a tuft of alpaca wool. She immediately passed it to William, saying, 'You need it more than me!'

When Things Go Wrong

The Queen famously described 1992 as her '*annus horribilis*'. The marriages of three of her four children were ending – the Prince and Princess of Wales announced their separation, as did the Duke and Duchess of York, while Princess Anne and Captain Mark Phillips actually divorced. The whole family had been the target of numerous media scandals, including the confirmation of a long-standing affair between Charles and his ex-girlfriend Camilla Parker Bowles, and then as the year was drawing to an end, the Queen's favoured home, Windsor Castle, was ravaged by fire.

Buckingham Palace press office also dismissed the rumours that Princess Anne was having an affair with Commander Tim Laurence as 'scurrilous, absurd and without foundation'. The couple were quietly married at Crathie Kirk, near Balmoral, in December 1992.

After her divorce from Prince Charles, Diana commented, 'People think that at the end of the day a man is the only answer. Actually, a fulfilling job is better for me.' She famously stated in a BBC *Panorama* interview, in November 1995, 'Well, there were three of us in this marriage, so it was a bit crowded.' She also said, 'Any sane person would have left long ago.' And Prince Charles? He said, 'Do you seriously expect me to be the first Prince of Wales in history not to have a mistress?'

Looking back on her marriage to Antony Armstrong-Jones, Princess Margaret reflected, 'Really, though, he was such a nice person in those days.' They had married in May 1960, but after their two children were born they led increasingly separate lives. After a series of revelations in the press, they formally separated in 1976 and divorced two years later.

Prince Andrew and Sarah Ferguson announced their separation in March 1992 and divorced in May 1996. Shortly after they separated, Sarah was asked how she was and replied in a typically jovial manner, 'I'm doing pretty well, considering. You know, in the past, when anyone left the Royal Family they had you beheaded.'

They shared custody of their two daughters and continued to share their marital home, Sunninghill Park, until 2004 when Andrew moved to the Royal Lodge in Windsor Great Park, Sarah later moving to the house next door. After a fire in her home in 2008, Sarah then moved in with Andrew. They continue to share the same house and be great friends, and periodically stories surface that they are about to remarry. Andrew described it as, 'Being divorced to, and not being divorced from.' Sarah adds, 'We like to say that we are the happiest divorced couple in the world.' Or to put it another way, 'We are the happiest unmarried couple.' She has also observed: 'He's a fantastic father and friend, and you cannot put Andrew and I in a box of any description.'

As Sarah Ferguson memorably commented, 'The men in this family are damn hard on their horses and their women.', 'I had to remember my place even though I was a redhead, Irish and a bit temperamental.' And 'I wanted to be perfect, but I should have just stayed this funny old thing.'

CHAPTER 2

Nearest and Dearest

Given their very public profile and the interest taken in their every move, the Royal Family are at their most relaxed and open with their nearest, though sometimes not so dearest.

'Monarchy involves the whole family, which means that different age groups are part of it. There are people who can look, for instance, at the Queen Mother and identify with that generation, or with us, or with our children,' Prince Philip said. He also reflected: 'The children soon discover that it's much safer to unburden yourself to a member of the family than just a friend … You see, you're never quite sure … a small indiscretion can lead to all sorts of difficulties.'

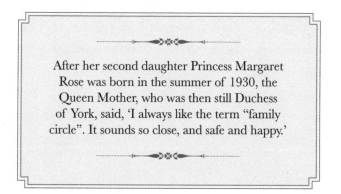

After her second daughter Princess Margaret Rose was born in the summer of 1930, the Queen Mother, who was then still Duchess of York, said, 'I always like the term "family circle". It sounds so close, and safe and happy.'

William says, 'It's like a rugby team. If you're picking for the World Cup final, you're picking experience with youth. Everything is better off having that balance and that mix. I think that, especially, goes for the monarchy.'

One's Family

When Philip proposed to Elizabeth at Balmoral in August 1946, she agreed immediately without consulting her parents first. Her father, King George VI, agreed to the engagement on the condition that they kept it secret until after her twenty-first birthday the following April, and a Royal Family tour of South Africa. It was Elizabeth's and Margaret's first overseas trip.

Following the public announcement of the wedding in November 1947, the King wrote to his daughter: 'I was so anxious for you to come to South Africa as you knew. Our family, us four, the "Royal Family", must remain together – with additions of course at suitable moments! I have watched you grow up all these years with pride under the skilful direction of Mummy, who as you know is the most marvellous person in the world in my eyes.'

Years later, when Queen, Elizabeth echoed her father when she said of the Queen Mother, 'She has been the most marvellous mother – always standing back and never interfering.'

Princess Margaret reckoned, 'In our family we don't have rifts. We have a jolly good row and then it's all over. And I've only twice ever had a row with my sister.' She never revealed what those two arguments were about.

Princess Anne commented that she learned at an early age to accept that her mother would sometimes be away from home, occasionally for weeks or even months on overseas visits. She accepted that it was all part of 'the service life' and 'not a personal thing'. She added, 'As all mothers, she's put up with a lot and we're still on speaking terms, so I think that's no mean feat.'

Looking at their family as a whole Anne said, 'Judging by some families I think we are all on pretty good speaking terms after all this time and that's no mean achievement for quite a lot of families.' And the Queen on her family dramas? 'Like all the best families, we have our share of eccentricities, of impetuous and wayward youngsters, and of family disagreements.'

Talking about their unique family position, William commented, 'As I learned from growing up, you don't mess with your grandmother.' He's also quoted saying, 'Being a small boy it's very daunting seeing the Queen around and not really quite knowing what to talk about.' And when Harry was advising a group of visitors to Buckingham Palace, he said, 'If you suddenly bump into her [the Queen] in the corridor, don't panic. I know you will. We all do.'

As they've grown older, both princes have found their relationship with the Queen has evolved. William explained, 'My relationship with my grandmother has gone from strength to strength. As a shy, younger man it could be harder to talk about weighty matters. It was: "This is my grandmother who is the Queen, and these are serious historical subjects."' And he tellingly added, 'When the Queen says "well done", it means so much.'

What's in a Name?

The Royal Family are fond of nicknames. As a small child, Elizabeth called her grandfather, King George V, 'Grandpapa England'. And her own (very young) grandson, William, gave the Queen an unlikely name. Falling over at Buckingham Palace he cried out, 'Gary, Gary!' As she hurried across to pick him up, a puzzled guest asked who was Gary, assuming it was someone in the royal household. 'Oh, I'm Gary,' the Queen explained. 'He hasn't learned to say Granny yet.'

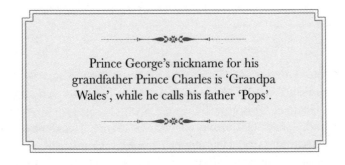

Prince George's nickname for his grandfather Prince Charles is 'Grandpa Wales', while he calls his father 'Pops'.

In a televised interview celebrating the Queen's ninetieth birthday, the Duchess of Cambridge revealed the family tradition was being continued. 'George is only two-and-a-half and he calls her Gan-Gan.' Kate added that the Queen was very much the doting great-grandmother, 'She always leaves a little gift or something in their room when we go and stay and that just shows her love for the family.'

The Queen's name for herself when she was a young child was 'Tillabet', later changed to 'Lilibet', an affectionate pet name that family and close friends still use, although Philip also calls his wife 'Sausage' and 'Cabbage'. Wallis Simpson, the catalyst for the abdication crisis of 1936, when King Edward VIII gave up the throne to marry 'the woman I love', nicknamed his young niece, Princess Elizabeth, 'Shirley Temple' and her mother 'Mrs Temple'. Princess Margaret's childhood name was 'Baba', while the Queen Mother was known as 'Merry Mischief' or 'Buffy', which was her brother David Bowes-Lyon's nickname for her. She and David, who were close in age, were also dubbed 'The two Benjamins'.

♛

Prince Charles and Camilla are rumoured to call each other 'Fred' and 'Gladys', and as a pupil at the Timbertop Campus of Geelong Grammar School in Victoria, Australia, where Charles spent two terms, he had the unflattering nickname 'Pommy Bastard'. He later described his experience at the school as character building and said he had loved his time there.

♛

Prince Andrew's nanny, Mabel Anderson, nicknamed her royal charge 'Baby Grumpling', while Andrew called both his nanny and his mother 'Mamba'. Staff at Buckingham Palace couldn't help but refer to the young Prince as 'Andy Pandy'.

Prince Philip had a rather surprising nickname for his second son. Play-fighting with him one bedtime, Philip was left with a black eye after Andrew scored a lucky punch. There was no disguising the bruising and when Philip arrived at a film premiere later that evening, he pointed to the shiner and said, 'That was The Boss.'

Later, Andrew often found himself following in his older brother's footsteps and was not best pleased when he was sometimes compared unfavourably. When he began serving on HMS *Hermes*, the aircraft carrier on which Charles had also served, and training at Dartmouth Naval College, he was nicknamed 'Action Man 2'.

Prince Edward occasionally used the name Mr Shakespeare to hide his real identity when flying, and on school trips travelled under the name 'Edward Bishop'. For a time while he was at Gordonstoun school, his nickname was 'Jaws' on account of his braces. His other nickname was 'Earl', an acronym taken from his full name, Edward Antony Richard Louis.

Married to the Queen's cousin, Prince Michael of Kent, Princess Michael is not afraid of voicing her opinions in public and once described herself as 'the thinking man's princess', Princess Diana as 'the beautiful Sloane princess' and Sarah Duchess of York as 'the Coronation Street princess'. Philip's nickname for Princess Michael was 'Motormouth', while Margaret, apparently not a fan, called her 'Princess Pushy'.

Prince William, whose friends generally call him 'Wills', was known as 'Steve' to provide a degree of anonymity when he was a student at St Andrews, while Harry referred to himself as 'Spike'. In his younger days, to avoid attention, Prince Charles would sign himself into clubs as 'Charlie Chester'.

As a small boy William was sometimes called 'The Tornado' by his family, possibly because, as Diana claimed, 'William is just like me – always in trouble.' Diana also called him 'Wombat' following a trip to Australia when he was two, 'Not because I look like a wombat,' William explained, before pausing, 'or maybe I do!'

Harry has a different explanation. 'He was still crawling at six.'

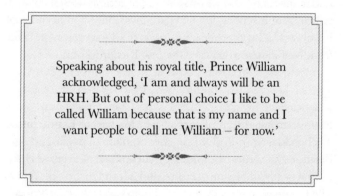

Speaking about his royal title, Prince William acknowledged, 'I am and always will be an HRH. But out of personal choice I like to be called William because that is my name and I want people to call me William – for now.'

When asked about nicknames for his brother, William joked, 'Oh, Ginger, whatever. You can call him whatever you want. Most of them … a bit rude.' And when asked if Harry phoned or texted very often, William added, 'It usually means he's left something at home and I have to bring it for him.'

When Prince George was a baby, he was referred to as 'PC' for Prince Cambridge, making Kate 'MC' or Mother Cambridge. Kate had her own nickname for a while as a child. The Middleton family had two pet guinea pigs called 'Pip' and 'Squeak'. As her sister is Pippa, Kate naturally became 'Squeak'.

♛

Shortly before the public announcement of his engagement to Elizabeth in July 1947, Philip adopted his uncle Louis Mountbatten's surname. Born a prince of Greece and Denmark, he was a member of the European House of Schleswig-Holstein-Sonderburg-Glücksburg. Not a name that rolls easily off the tongue, and at the time it was also considered far too Germanic for post-war Britain.

When Elizabeth became Queen in 1952 she promised Philip that their children would keep his surname, but she came under mounting pressure from Prime Minister Winston Churchill and her formidable grandmother, Queen Mary. Young and inexperienced in matters of state, the Queen reluctantly gave in to their demands and agreed that her children and future grandchildren would all take the surname Windsor. Philip was furious, ranting, 'I'm nothing but a bloody amoeba.' And, 'I am the only man in the country not allowed to give his name to his children.'

Never comfortable with the decision she had made, in 1960 the Queen announced that any of her direct descendants who did not hold the title of Prince or Princess would be called Mountbatten-Windsor.

Royal Babies

In July 2013, with the birth of her first great-grandchild expected any day, the Queen laughed, 'I hope it arrives soon because I'm going on holiday.' She had been more circumspect on the possible arrival date of Andrew and Sarah's first child, her granddaughter Beatrice in 1988, observing, 'Babies come when they are ready; they don't come to order.' But even she grew impatient complaining, 'I'm getting fed up waiting for it to arrive.'

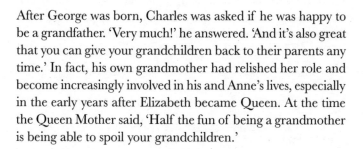

After George was born, Charles was asked if he was happy to be a grandfather. 'Very much!' he answered. 'And it's also great that you can give your grandchildren back to their parents any time.' In fact, his own grandmother had relished her role and become increasingly involved in his and Anne's lives, especially in the early years after Elizabeth became Queen. At the time the Queen Mother said, 'Half the fun of being a grandmother is being able to spoil your grandchildren.'

Interviewed after completing the London Marathon in April 2012, Harry promised that Will and Kate would run in the next one. When he was asked what happened to them after the race in 2013, Harry joked, 'He's old. She's pregnant.'

When Charles was born in November 1948, Princess Elizabeth (as she was then) sounded every bit the proud new mother. 'I still can't believe he is really mine, but perhaps that happens to new parents. Anyway, this particular boy's parents couldn't be more proud of him.'

Philip's verdict on his new-born son was that 'he looks like a plum pudding.' Meanwhile Princess Margaret quipped, 'I suppose I'll now be known as Charley's aunt.' She also said, of her own children, they 'are not royal; they just happen to have the Queen for their aunt.'

With the arrival of a daughter in 1950, Elizabeth got into the habit of taking both children to the park, pushing Anne in a pram. The dogs naturally came, too. 'My corgis have become pram-minded. They pay more attention to the pram than me. They know it means a walk,' the young mother observed.

Prince Philip said of his baby daughter, 'It's the sweetest girl.' He also commented on the constant gurgling sounds she made when tiny: 'We have a budding opera singer in the family.'

When Charles was born, Philip passed the time by playing squash with his private secretary. It's strange now to think that this was quite normal for the time. Along with most modern fathers, Charles was present for the birth of both his sons, likewise William and Harry.

During Andrew's birth in 1960, Philip stepped in to give the speech the Queen should have made at a Guildhall lunch, quipping, 'It is, of course, a matter of great regret to us all that the Queen cannot be here today but, as you realize, she has other matters to attend to.' After the birth, Philip was typically understated, 'People want their first child very much. They want the second almost as much. If a third child comes along they accept it as natural, but they haven't gone out of their way to try and get it. […] When the fourth child comes along, in most cases it's unintentional.'

Edward's birth on 10 March 1964 at Buckingham Palace was the only one of his children's births that Philip attended, a sign of the social changes happening in the 1960s and the Queen's specific invitation. After Edward's christening at St George's Chapel, Windsor Castle, the Queen said that he was 'the quietest of my children'. A few years later, his grandmother the Queen Mother took him to his first classical music concert and remarked, 'I have never known a child to sit so still.'

The royal photographer, Cecil Beaton, took the first official photos of Edward four years later. Looking through the prints, the Queen commented, 'It's most unfortunate that all my sons have such long eyelashes while my daughter hasn't any at all.'

When Prince William was born on 21 June 1982, Charles sounded like any new father having witnessed the birth of their first child: 'It was rather a grown-up thing. I found it rather a shock to my system.' Probably not as much as his wife did. Diana admitted, 'No one told me it would be like this.' She also said, 'I felt the whole country was in labour with me.' She later added, 'If men had to have babies they would only have one each.' And speaking of motherhood, 'It's hard work and no pay. I couldn't cope with a brace.'

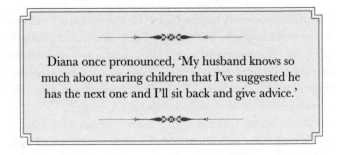

Diana once pronounced, 'My husband knows so much about rearing children that I've suggested he has the next one and I'll sit back and give advice.'

Asked how he felt by the crowd and press waiting outside St Mary's Hospital, Paddington, for news of the baby, Charles said he was, 'relieved … delighted … overwhelmed … over the moon'. And on the question of William's appearance, 'He looks marvellous. Fair, sort of blondish. He's not bad …' whereupon a well-wisher shouted out: 'Nice one, Charlie! Let's have another one!' The Prince's quick reply was, 'Bloody hell! Give us a chance. Ask my wife. I don't think she'd be too pleased yet.'

When William was a few months old, Charles was asked what he was like: 'He's not at all shy. He's a great grinner, but he does dribble a lot.' 'He's just like his father,' joked Diana.

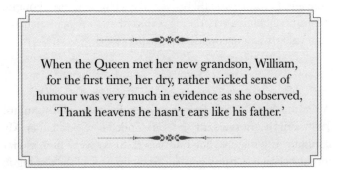

When the Queen met her new grandson, William, for the first time, her dry, rather wicked sense of humour was very much in evidence as she observed, 'Thank heavens he hasn't ears like his father.'

Like his father before him, William was christened in the Music Room at Buckingham Palace. And, following family tradition, he wore the christening gown originally made for Queen Victoria's first child, Victoria, in 1841. William cried throughout the short service until his mother gave him her little finger to suck. 'He's a good speech-maker,' smiled the Queen.

When Harry was born on 15 September 1984, Charles exclaimed, 'Oh God, it's a boy! And he's even got red hair!' Princess Diana was said not to be best pleased at this reaction. She also thought that 'hugs can do great amounts of good – especially for children'.

Princess Anne told her husband Mark Phillips, 'Honestly, three-day eventing at Burghley is a doddle compared to this.' She had just given birth to their first son, Peter, on 15 November 1977. She waited four years before having Zara (born on 15 May 1981), her name suggested by Charles. It means 'bright as the dawn,' Anne explained. 'The baby made a somewhat positive arrival and my brother thought that Zara was an appropriate name ... I heard from just about every Zara in Britain at the time and I promise you there are quite a few.' She also thought, 'Being pregnant is a very boring six months. I am not particularly maternal. It's an occupational hazard of being a wife.'

After the birth of his first daughter, Beatrice, on 8 August 1988, Prince Andrew said, 'It feels wonderful to be a father. My daughter is gorgeous, but I'm biased. She is very pretty.' Her mother claimed, 'She's got Andrew's lips' and 'She's going to be a carrot-top just like me ... It's only a tinge of hair so far, but it's quite clearly the same colour as my own.' She also said, 'She's just incredibly placid and calm, sleeps through the night. I don't know where she gets it from, probably her father.' She's also on record adding, 'I hate grownups and love children.'

When his own first child was born on 22 July 2013, Prince William couldn't resist joking that his baby son had 'got way more hair than me, thank God.' He also said, 'He's got [Kate's] looks, thankfully.' And, just like any other new father:

> There are times where you can't do it yourself and the system takes over, or it's appropriate to do things differently. But I think driving your son and your wife away from hospital was really important to me.
>
> I think the last few weeks for me have been just a very different emotional experience. Something I never thought I would feel myself. And I find … a lot of things affect me differently now. As any new parent knows, you're only too happy to show off your new child and, you know, proclaim that he is the best looking or the best everything.

A few weeks on and the pressures of being a first-time parent are the same even if you happen to be royal. 'I have to say that I thought search-and-rescue duties over Snowdonia were physically and mentally demanding, but looking after a three-week-old baby is up there!' William also reflected, 'I'm a lot more emotional than I used to be. I never used to get too wound up or worried about things. But now the smallest little things, you well up a little more, you get affected by the sort of things that happen around the world or whatever a lot more, I think, as a father.'

While visiting a London primary school in 2017, Kate reflected on the way she had been brought up. 'My parents taught me about the importance of qualities like kindness, respect and honesty. And I realize how central values like these have been to me throughout my life.' She went on to talk about how she and William hoped to pass on these same core values to their own children. 'In my view they are just as important as excelling in maths or sport.'

With the impending birth of their first child, Prince Harry and Meghan decided to break with royal protocol by not appointing the Royal Household gynaecologists who usually attend all royal labours and who supervised the births of his brother's three children. Meghan opted instead for a female-led team because she did not want 'the men in suits' present. A Palace source was quoted saying, 'She was adamant that she wanted her own people. It did leave a few of us a little baffled.'

Harry, playing to the audience on a trip to Morocco with his wife in February 2019, couldn't resist a bad joke after well-wishers congratulated the couple on their pregnancy. 'What?!' Harry exclaimed turning to Meghan in mock shock. 'You're pregnant?' 'Surprise!' laughed his wife. But Harry pushed it just a little further, 'Is it mine?'

Born early on 6 May 2019, Bank Holiday Monday, Archie didn't make his first public appearance until a couple of days later. An overwhelmed and ecstatic Harry said outside his new family home, Frogmore Cottage, Windsor, 'It's been the most amazing experience I could ever have possibly imagined … How any woman does what they do is beyond comprehension. We're both absolutely thrilled and so grateful for all the love and support from everybody out there. It's been amazing, so we just want to share this with everybody.'

Like any new father he was slightly dazed by the experience and couldn't stop smiling. He joked, 'I haven't been at many births! This is definitely my first birth. It was amazing, absolutely incredible.' And, 'As every father or parent would say … [the] … baby is absolutely amazing. But this little thing is absolutely to die for, so I am just over the moon.' So over the moon was Harry he even appeared to thank the horses watching from their stables behind him.

On hearing the news, William was delighted, only half joking when he said, 'I'm very pleased and glad to welcome my own brother into the sleep deprivation society that is parenting.' Some things remain the same whether you're royal or not. When asked if he had any pearls of wisdom for his younger brother, given his own experience as a father of three, William laughed, 'Plenty of advice, plenty of advice, but no – I wish him all the best …'

There was some amusing confusion about Archie's arrival, with reports saying he was the first son of the Duke and Duchess of Cambridge, rather than Sussex, before the blunder was spotted and quickly corrected.

William and Kate were at the launch of the King's Cup Regatta in Greenwich when they heard of the birth. Asked about his new nephew, William said, 'Yes, absolutely, I'm an uncle, second time for me …' he paused before pointing to his wife, 'and you as well.' The couple already had one nephew, Kate's sister's son Arthur, born in October 2018. Kate laughingly retorted, 'I'm definitely not an uncle.'

The Queen and Prince Philip, attending an Order of Merit lunch at Windsor Castle shortly after the birth of their latest grandson, smiled warmly in agreement when asked, 'Life is good for Your Majesty?'

Ask the Family

If you want an honest opinion, who do you ask? Family members can always be relied upon not to pull any punches and to be brutally honest about each other. In this, the royals are no different from anyone else.

It's not wholly surprising that Prince Philip has a tendency to tell it as he sees it. And, after more than seventy years in the public eye, he is used to playing to the crowd. As someone who likes to make the most of any situation, he enjoys raising a laugh, sometimes at somebody else's expense.

In 1991, Philip decided it was time to give up playing polo. He was interviewed by veteran broadcaster Terry Wogan who commented on the rather athletic, high-speed nature of the sport. Philip replied, 'There comes a time in your life when you don't want to be so athletic any more, I can tell you.'

Wogan then mentioned that Charles was still playing polo. Philip grinned, responding, 'He's still young and vigorous … He's younger than I am, funnily enough.' Warming to the audience's obvious appreciation, he added, 'He may not look it …' before roaring with laughter.

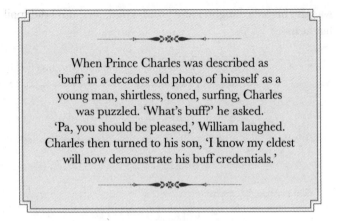

When Prince Charles was described as
'buff' in a decades old photo of himself as a
young man, shirtless, toned, surfing, Charles
was puzzled. 'What's buff?' he asked.
'Pa, you should be pleased,' William laughed.
Charles then turned to his son, 'I know my eldest
will now demonstrate his buff credentials.'

Acknowledging some of the trickier aspects of his relationship with his eldest son, Philip commented, 'He's a romantic and I'm a pragmatist. That means we do see things differently … And because I don't see things as a romantic would, I'm unfeeling.' He also said of Charles, 'He has no interest in things, but all the more for persons.'

Speaking in 1970 about his then twenty-year-old daughter Princess Anne, a keen horsewoman, Philip said, 'If it doesn't fart or eat hay, she isn't interested.' The Queen also joked in a similar vein when Anne and Captain Mark Phillips married in 1973, 'I expect their children will be four-legged.'

After a foiled kidnap attempt on the Princess in March 1974, her father's verdict was, 'If the man had succeeded in abducting Anne, she would have given him a hell of a time while in captivity.' Philip saw a kindred spirit in his daughter and always appreciated her feisty, no-nonsense approach. She was also his only daughter and he admitted, 'Perhaps I did spoil her at times.'

> Referring to the press, Princess Anne said, 'They are always waiting for me to put my foot in it, just like my father.'

The Duke and Duchess of York's new home at Sunninghill Park came in for a great deal of criticism when it was completed in 1990. Often jokingly referred to as 'South York' – referring to 'Southfork', the huge, plain, functional ranch at the centre of the popular TV series *Dallas* – Prince Philip was equally dismissive: 'It looks like a tart's bedroom.' And he didn't stop there.

After the couple's divorce, Philip did a double take at a Guards' Polo Club reception in 2001. 'Good God! I can't take canapés from you – you're Fergie!' he barked at a startled red-haired waitress. He laughingly explained, 'She's working anywhere for money now.'

When Prince Edward was offered a place at Jesus College, Cambridge, to read history, in spite of his less than glittering A-level grades, his father is said to have joked, 'What a friend we have in Jesus!'

After graduating in 1986, Edward joined the Royal Marines, a long-held ambition, and indeed the Marines had contributed towards his tuition at university on condition of his future service. He was enthusiastic: 'The Marines are looking forward to having me if only to rub my nose in it. Everybody thinks I'm mad. It's probably the greatest challenge I will ever have to meet.'

A few months later, after completing just a third of the training, Edward dropped out. At the time he explained, 'It was a very agonizing decision … But having got here I changed my mind and decided that the services generally – not just the Royal Marines – was not the career I wanted.' Asked what his youngest son was planning next, Philip simply said, 'Heaven knows.'

Perhaps less than appreciative of Edward's subsequent career in the world of entertainment, Philip joked to fellow guests at William's twenty-first birthday party after the 'comedy terrorist' Aaron Barschak had been arrested for gate-crashing the event wearing a pink dress, fake beard and turban, that Edward must have planned the intrusion. He was the only one of the senior family members not present and Philip reasoned, 'It's bound to have been Edward. Only that boy could have coached such a rotten performance out of someone.'

The Joke's on Me

She may be Queen but that has never stopped her family from teasing her. When still a Princess, Elizabeth joined the Women's Auxiliary Territorial Service in spring 1944. She learned to drive and was very proud of her newfound skills servicing cars and lorries, changing tyres and spark plugs. When her parents visited the training centre, Elizabeth was filmed working on a Red Cross lorry. When they returned some time later, King George asked his daughter, 'Haven't you got it mended yet?' He then revealed he had sabotaged her work by removing the distributor.

Prince Andrew remembers: 'At a family dinner, she [the Queen] stood to go, and the footman very properly pulled her chair away. At that moment I asked her a question and she sat down again, except there was no chair. Everyone, including the Queen, laughed and laughed.'

Prince William confessed, 'I'm probably a bit of a cheeky grandson, like my brother as well. We both tend to take the mickey a bit too much.' One Christmas, Harry is said to have given his grandmother a shower cap emblazoned with the caption, 'Ain't Life a Bitch'.

The Queen Mother was well aware of her reputation in the media for enjoying a glass or two. Served a rather meagre measure of gin, she asked for more, laughing, 'I've got my reputation to think of.' And before leaving for an outdoor lunch party that she was perhaps not looking forward to, she left a note for a member of her personal staff: 'I think that I will take two small bottles of Dubonnet and gin with me this morning, in case it is needed.'

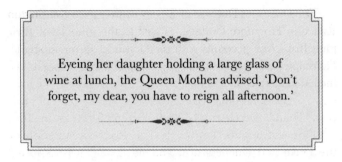

Eyeing her daughter holding a large glass of wine at lunch, the Queen Mother advised, 'Don't forget, my dear, you have to reign all afternoon.'

And while on the subject, watching Philip down his third champagne cocktail at a reception, Elizabeth remarked a touch frostily, 'What kind of speech do you think you are going to make now?'

As a mild dig at the Queen's uncle, the Duke of Windsor, who abdicated the throne to marry American divorcee, Wallis Simpson, Prince Philip told an audience in England, 'People think there's a rigid class system here, but dukes have been known to marry chorus girls. Some have even married Americans.'

Royal Rivalries

A great deal has been written about the supposed rivalry between the Duchess of Cambridge and the Duchess of Sussex, or maybe the rift is actually between the two brothers, William and Harry. Whether real or a confection, the stories have gathered pace with royal watchers scrutinizing body language and every nuance of behaviour.

The Duke and Duchess of Sussex's move from Kensington Palace to Frogmore Cottage, as well as the splitting of their joint Instagram accounts with the Cambridges remaining @KensingtonRoyal and the Sussexes launching @SussexRoyal, fuelled headlines of 'Friction between the Fab Four'. There is now speculation about what lies behind the division of their Royal Foundation charity, which was originally set up in 2009.

This will now be known as The Royal Foundation of the Duke and Duchess of Cambridge, and it is expected that the Duke and Duchess of Sussex will establish a new charity although the couples will continue to work together on initiatives such as their mental health campaign. Buckingham Palace has reminded the media that senior royals have historically always set up their own households on marriage and this was always the plan for Prince Harry. It also follows that, as the heirs to the throne, it is appropriate that William and Kate take increasingly prominent roles and that Harry and Meghan concentrate on different areas.

This is not the only royal rivalry over the years. As the younger son, it was usually Prince Andrew who resented the attention heaped upon his older brother, especially as Andrew was always the second to do anything and was constantly being compared unfavourably. However, there was a point when the media began to focus on his good looks and 'Randy Andy' image. 'My only vice is women,' Andrew said at the time. When asked about his brother, Charles's acid response was, 'Ah, the one with the Robert Redford looks.'

Much was made in the press about the supposed rivalry between Princess Diana and Sarah Ferguson. Diana told her biographer, Andrew Morton, that Sarah 'wooed everybody in this family and did it so well. She left me looking like dirt.' She added that Charles had even remarked, 'I wish you would be like Fergie – all jolly.' And to a group of photographers Diana said, 'You won't need me any more, now you've got Fergie.'

Sarah didn't see it that way, though: 'Diana was always the saint, the tall, beautiful figure, and I was always this sinner with a rather large bottom.'

Sarah also commented, 'It was very difficult when everyone looked at Diana as the most beautiful with the fantastically fabulous figure and then they'd go, "Oh yes, and her." It was always this feeling when you go to the gym. She's in Lycra and I'm in *Chariots of Fire* shorts.'

However, as their marriages fell apart the pair increasingly leaned upon one another. Sarah wrote, 'We burned the phone wires into the night, trading secrets and jokes that no one else would understand.' 'I used to call her Dutch as in Duchess before she got married to Charles,' she remembered. 'There was no woman with a better sense of humour than Diana … She was very clever. She'd been in the Royal Family a bit longer than me so she always knew the tricks. She knew that if she ran quicker to dinner than I did, she wouldn't have to sit next to somebody who was rather difficult. After a few years, we would see who could run down the corridor quicker.'

Rivalry was one thing but when it came to Princess Margaret, feuds could last for years. Diana and Margaret seemed to understand each other, until it became obvious that Diana had collaborated closely on Andrew Morton's biography. Margaret did not approve and sent her a furious note. After Diana's BBC interview with Martin Bashir was broadcast in November 1995, Margaret then totally ignored her, not an easy feat as they continued to live in adjacent apartments in Kensington Palace, though Margaret had years of practice ignoring Princess Michael, her other neighbour.

A National Treasure

The Queen Mother and the Queen used to exchange humorous verses – witty ditties they would send back and forth to amuse each other, especially when they were off duty in Scotland and had more time. Before *Britannia* was decommissioned in 1997, the Queen regularly sailed from Balmoral to Castle Mey, her mother's home in Caithness, and she composed one such verse to thank her mother for dinner:

A meal of such splendour, repast of such zest,
It will take us to Sunday just to digest.

Prince Charles always got on exceptionally well with his grandmother and was lavish in his praise: 'Ever since I can remember, my grandmother has been a most wonderful example of fun, laughter and warmth, and above all, exquisite taste in so many things. For me she has always been one of those extraordinary, rare people whose touch can turn everything to gold … She belongs to the priceless brand of human beings whose greatest gift is to enhance life for others through her own effervescent enthusiasm for life.'

The Queen Mother said of herself,
'I'm not as nice as you think I am.'

Princess Anne's view of her relationship with the Queen Mother was more circumspect: 'There is rather a special relationship between the eldest grandson and a grandmother, I think, which is not true of granddaughters.'

The Queen Mother had a reputation for tardiness, a trait that her formidable father-in-law, King George V, usually loathed. He insisted on punctuality but was so impressed with his 'charming' daughter-in-law that she was the one person for whom he would make an exception. 'If she weren't late she would be perfect, and how horrible that would be,' he said, telling his son, 'The better I know and the more I see of your dear little wife, the more charming I think she is and everyone falls in love with her.'

On her own lack of punctuality, the Queen Mother said, 'It's much more important not to miss anyone than to be five minutes late.' But she also acknowledged that, 'traditions exist to be kept'.

Ever tactful, the Queen Mother's usual way of saying no was, 'Perhaps another time.' She referred to her wardrobe as 'my props' and developed her own immediately recognizable style of dress. When a designer suggested some alternatives the Queen Mother was polite in her refusal, 'They are absolutely charming – but I think these are even more delightful.'

Speaking in 2002 after the death of their great-grandmother, the Queen Mother, at the grand old age of 101, William and Harry remembered a surprising scene at Sandringham when the family had gathered together for the holidays.

William began, 'It was two or three Christmases ago and we were sitting down watching Ali G on television. We were laughing when [the Queen Mother] came in. She couldn't understand what was going on, so we explained. She saw Ali G click his fingers and say "respeck", and Harry and I showed her what to do. She loved it, and after three goes she had it.'

When Christmas Day arrived, she was keen to try out her new impression on the rest of the family. Harry said: 'It was at the end of the meal, and she stood up and said, "Darling, lunch was marvellous – respeck", and clicked her fingers.' William added, 'She loved a good laugh, even if the joke was about her … Anything that was meant to be formal and went wrong she enjoyed. She would have a good giggle. She had such a young sense of humour. Every single thing that went wrong or was funny for any reason she laughed herself stupid about – it kept us all sane.'

He also revealed that before he left for university in 2001, his great-grandmother told him, 'Any good parties, invite me down.' 'I said yes, but there was no way. I knew full well that if I invited her down she would dance me under the table.'

Whatever the ups and downs of their family relationships over the years, there can be no doubting the strong bonds and genuine affection for one another that the Royal Family share. One of the most poignant comments on love and loss came from the Queen Mother shortly after the death of her husband, George VI. They had been married for almost twenty-nine years and he was just fifty-six years old. 'One must feel gratitude for what has been rather than distress for what is lost.' As the Queen said, 'Grief is the price we pay for love.'

CHAPTER 3

In the Line of
Duty

The Queen Mother once remarked, 'The work you do is the rent you pay for the room you occupy on earth.' And her work ethic and sense of duty is one that the Royal Family has taken to heart. Her daughter is still working after almost seventy years on the throne, with just the slightest reduction in duties as a concession to age after turning ninety. Prince Philip, her consort and constant companion on state occasions and tours, finally retired from official engagements at the age of ninety-six in 2017.

When asked if she proposed slowing down at all, having passed her sixtieth birthday, Princess Anne pointed to the example set by her parents and grandmother: 'Look around at other members of my family who are considerably older than me, and tell me whether they've set an example that makes you think I might. Unlikely.'

Now approaching seventy, her attitude has not changed. 'It's just another birthday.'

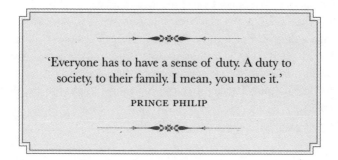

'Everyone has to have a sense of duty. A duty to society, to their family. I mean, you name it.'

PRINCE PHILIP

Prince William provides another perspective. 'All these questions about do you want to be king?' he explained. 'It's not a question of wanting to be, it's something I was born into and it's my duty ... Wanting is not the right word. But those stories about me not wanting to be king are all wrong.'

Pomp and Circumstance

At Queen Elizabeth's coronation on 2 June 1953, Westminster Abbey was packed with 8,000 guests. Millions more watched on television sets around the world. But what none of them heard was the young Queen's question – 'Ready girls?!' – to her six Coronation Maids of Honour, nor her frantic whisper to Archbishop Geoffrey Fisher to 'Get me started!' She needed a good push to get going as friction between the heavy state robes and the thick carpet had her firmly fixed to the spot.

Interviewed by Alastair Bruce for a BBC documentary in 2018, she explained, 'I remember one moment when I was going against the pile of the carpet and I couldn't move at all.' She added, 'Yes, they hadn't thought of that.'

Displaying a dry sense of humour, she also appeared to take a dim view of famous footage of her then small children, Charles and Anne. The siblings were captured on film playing under her gown's 21-foot train when the royal party returned to Buckingham Palace after the ceremony. 'Such fun for the children,' Bruce quipped. 'Not what they're meant to do,' the Queen replied, with a hint of a smile.

As the day of the coronation approached, the young Queen found her confidence growing. 'Extraordinary thing, I no longer feel anxious or worried – but I have lost all my timidity.' She was only twenty-seven. She refused the offer of a break to rest halfway through the lengthy ceremony, claiming, 'I'll be all right. I'm as strong as a horse.'

Philip was the first to pay homage to his newly crowned Sovereign, solemnly promising, 'I, Philip, Duke of Edinburgh, do become your liege man of life and limb, and of earthly worship; and faith and truth I will bear unto you, to live and die, against all manner of folks. So help me God.' On leaving the Abbey at the end of the service, Philip couldn't resist joking to his wife, 'Where did you get that hat?'

Asked about the ceremonial trappings of monarchy, Prince Charles said, 'I would change nothing. Besides ceremony being a major and important aspect of monarchy, something that has grown and developed over a thousand years in Britain, I happen to enjoy it enormously.'

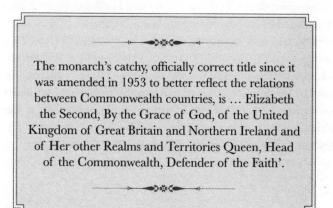

The monarch's catchy, officially correct title since it was amended in 1953 to better reflect the relations between Commonwealth countries, is … Elizabeth the Second, By the Grace of God, of the United Kingdom of Great Britain and Northern Ireland and of Her other Realms and Territories Queen, Head of the Commonwealth, Defender of the Faith'.

And on the subject of monarchy, Charles was candid: 'Something as curious as the monarchy won't survive unless you take account of people's attitudes. After all, if people don't want it, they won't have it.'

Speaking as Sovereign, the Queen claimed, 'The British Constitution has always been puzzling and always will be.' On America – 'We lost the American colonies because we lacked the statesmanship to know the right time and manner of yielding what is impossible to keep.' On progress – 'The upward course of a nation's history is due in the long run to the soundness of heart of its average men and women.' And on the Commonwealth – 'It is easy enough to define what the Commonwealth is not. Indeed, this is quite a popular pastime.'

Royal Weddings

When four-year-old William was chosen to be one of the page boys at Andrew's wedding to Sarah Ferguson in July 1986, Diana was a little nervous about how he would behave. 'I'm going to put down a line of Smarties in the aisle of Westminster Abbey so that William will know where to stand – and he's got to stay there …' She added, 'He's terribly excited. I only hope he behaves in the Abbey. He will rise to the occasion – at least I hope he will.' After the ceremony Diana could breathe a sigh of relief, 'I'm glad he behaved himself, because he can be a bit of a prankster.'

Prince William's wedding to Catherine Middleton took place on 29 April 2011 at Westminster Abbey. Although every bit a royal wedding, with all the pomp and ceremony that entails, it was also a very personal occasion. Before the wedding, William and Kate spoke to the Queen about what they wanted and she effectively told them to 'tear up the wedding plan' and organize it as they liked, although she was involved in every element.

The guest list included many of William and Kate's friends and contemporaries, as well as representatives from the Prince's charities. As a result, places were limited so ambassadors were included but their partners were not. Even the Queen and Prince Philip's guest numbers were limited to forty. The 1,900 invitations to Westminster Abbey came from the Queen rather than Prince Charles, and 650 guests were invited to a midday reception at Buckingham Palace where champagne and canapés were served instead of the more traditional wedding breakfast.

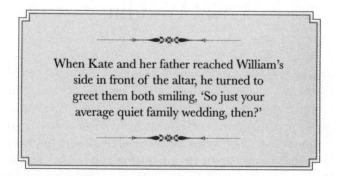

When Kate and her father reached William's side in front of the altar, he turned to greet them both smiling, 'So just your average quiet family wedding, then?'

Amongst the grandeur and spectacle, it was also a very intimate, heartfelt ceremony. Kate followed tradition and had the key four ingredients: something old – some of the lace on her Alexander McQueen wedding dress was antique; something new – her diamond earrings were a gift from her parents, designed by Robinson Pelham to include oak leaves and acorns representing the Middleton family crest; something borrowed – when your new grandmother-in-law is the Queen with an array of crown jewels at her disposal, why wouldn't you borrow the Cambridge Lover's Knot tiara for the big day; and something blue – designer Sarah Burton sewed a blue ribbon inside the dress.

As a tribute to her new husband, Sweet William flowers were included in Kate's small, fragrant bouquet. It also contained hyacinths, lilies of the valley and myrtle, following the royal wedding tradition, with a sprig from Queen Victoria's myrtle bush that she planted at Osborne House in 1845.

The Queen wore her grandmother Queen Mary's True Lover's Knot diamond brooch. She had previously worn the bow-shaped pin to Princess Margaret's wedding in 1960.

Out and About

When eighty-nine in 2015, still working hard and travelling the globe, the Queen could be forgiven for feeling a trifle sensitive about her advancing years. In Malta for a meeting of the Commonwealth Heads of Government, Canadian Prime Minister Justin Trudeau warmly welcomed her in his speech, praising Elizabeth for her 'long and tireless service'. Beginning her reply, the Queen joked, 'Thank you, Mister Prime Minister, for making me feel so old.'

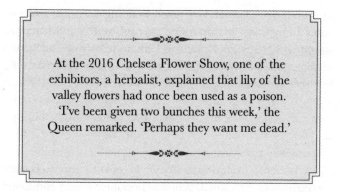

At the 2016 Chelsea Flower Show, one of the
exhibitors, a herbalist, explained that lily of the
valley flowers had once been used as a poison.
'I've been given two bunches this week,' the
Queen remarked. 'Perhaps they want me dead.'

A year later, when she had passed the milestone of her ninetieth
birthday, the Queen visited Northern Ireland. Deputy Minister
Martin McGuinness was given slightly short shrift when he
enquired about Her Majesty's health. 'Well, I'm alive anyway,'
was her somewhat cryptic reply.

All the Royal Family enjoy joking and this often involves mimicry.
Once when Prince Charles and the Queen were driving to the
Ascot races in an open carriage, there was a loud shout from
the crowd. Charles did not hear what was said and asked his
mother. 'Gizza wave, Liz!' the Queen replied in her best south
London accent, waving obligingly at the spectators.

The Queen and Prince Philip long ago christened the line of
dignitaries and worthies who frequently greet them on any royal
visit as 'the Chain Gang', a reference to the ceremonial robes,
hats and chains often worn by mayors, sheriffs and their deputies.

Philip also remarked, 'Occasionally I get fed up, going to visit a factory, when I am being shown around by the chairman who clearly hasn't got a clue and I try to get hold of the factory manager, but I can't because the chairman wants to make sure he's the one in all the photographs.'

♛

Prince Philip has opened countless new buildings, headquarters and charitable organizations, and knows the form of such occasions better than anyone. In one of his last public engagements before his retirement, he opened a new £25 million stand at the MCC's Lord's Cricket Ground. Before pulling the cord to draw aside the blue curtains he joked to onlookers, 'You're about to see the world's most experienced plaque-unveiler.'

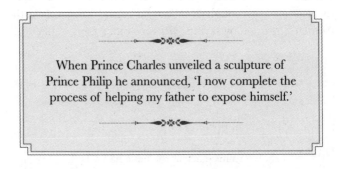

When Prince Charles unveiled a sculpture of Prince Philip he announced, 'I now complete the process of helping my father to expose himself.'

In 2003, revealing a plaque at the University of Hertfordshire's new Hatfield Campus, Philip cracked another joke. 'During the Blitz a lot of shops had their windows blown in and sometimes they put up notices saying, "More open than usual." I now declare this place more open than usual.'

And further back, in 1958, at the opening of an extension to Heriot-Watt College in Edinburgh, the lift containing the royal party got stuck between two floors. This was a gift for Philip who found the situation hilarious. 'This could only happen in a technical college,' he laughed.

Prince Philip is also infamous for a dubious joke to a group of deaf children standing near a steel drum band. 'Deaf? If you are near there, no wonder you are deaf.'

And there's more … At the fiftieth anniversary of the Duke of Edinburgh Awards scheme in September 2006, he declared, 'Young people are the same as they always were. They are just as ignorant.' He also quipped to a driving instructor in Scotland, 'How do you keep the natives off the booze long enough to pass the test?'

Recognizing his tendency to say the wrong thing, he once sensibly explained, 'It's my custom to say something flattering to begin with so I shall be excused if I put my foot in it later on.' Not always, though. In 1966, he began his speech to the Women's Institute by saying, 'British women can't cook.'

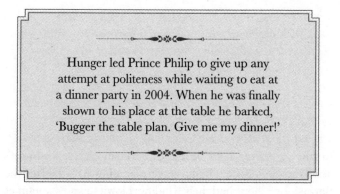

Hunger led Prince Philip to give up any attempt at politeness while waiting to eat at a dinner party in 2004. When he was finally shown to his place at the table he barked, 'Bugger the table plan. Give me my dinner!'

From Philip's abundant list of gaffes, we must include his meeting German Chancellor Helmut Kohl in 1997. Philip addressed him as 'Reichskanzler', a title last used by Adolph Hitler. In 2002, during a royal visit to Australia, the Queen and Philip were taken to some caves. Warned to watch out for the drips, he said breezily, 'Oh, I've run into plenty in my life.' And on the same tour, when visiting the Aboriginal Cultural Park in Queensland, he asked Aboriginal leader and successful entrepreneur William Brin, 'Do you still throw spears at each other?'

♛

Like father, like son: congratulating a beauty queen at a pageant in England a young Prince Charles said, 'My father told me that if I ever met a lady in a dress like yours, I must look her straight in the eyes.' And when Prince Harry joked with a class of fourteen- to fifteen-year-old junior high school pupils during a visit to the US, he asked, 'Who's the best pupil? I was always the worst!'

♛

Camilla also likes a quip. On English students – 'They don't spend much time on their studies. They're more interested in partying and having fun.' On a royal visit to the set of TV soap opera *Coronation Street*, she took a turn behind the bar at the Rover's Return – 'I hope I'm not going to spill it. Who is going to drink this afterwards? Any takers?' And from January 2010, when she joined Age Concern's staff, volunteers and supporters at RAF Lyneham in Wiltshire to celebrate the charity's sixtieth anniversary – 'Sixty is a milestone in anyone's life as those of us who have already reached it know only too well.' But the next part of her speech was a tad iffy. 'Since the charity was established in 1949, thousands of elderly people in Wiltshire have benefited from its many services ranging from home support to luncheon and technology clubs and toenail cutting, which I am very interested by.'

The Royal Yacht

When Prince Charles suggested including a visit to Gibraltar on his honeymoon cruise with Diana on board *Britannia*, there was some concern that this could cause controversy as Spain was then loudly disputing Britain's claim to the Overseas Territory. The Queen was forthright in her reply: 'He's my son, it's my yacht, and it's my colony!'

Her yacht, yes, but who paid for the upkeep? In service from 1954 when the Queen and Philip returned from their six-month tour of the Commonwealth, by 1961 *Britannia* was in need of repair. When details of the planned refit at a cost of a then whopping £2 million were made known, there was outrage in the press. The Queen had known nothing about the proposals and summoned the First Lord of the Admiralty, Lord Carrington, for an explanation. He said that as *Britannia* was owned by the state, the admiralty division of the Ministry of Defence would foot the bill. 'I see,' Her Majesty replied. 'You pay and I get the blame.'

Meeting the Public

The Queen Mother loved her royal duties and relished the variety of people she was introduced to over the years. 'I love meeting people,' she once asserted. 'I have met people of every possible kind and it is so easy to get on with them after the first moment, isn't it? Nearly everyone is so pleasant. When one is eighteen, one has very definite dislikes, but as one grows older one becomes more tolerant and finds that nearly everyone is, in some degree, nice.'

As royalty, the family meet everyone from presidents and heads of state to the average man or woman in the street. It's hard to imagine a time when the royals did not meet and greet the public, but it was Queen Elizabeth who broke with tradition to make it the norm. During a state tour of Australia and New Zealand with Philip in 1970, she suggested that instead of meeting only officials she wanted an opportunity to talk to those in the crowd. The experiment was a big success. The 'walkabout', as it was immediately christened, has remained a feature of royal visits at home and abroad ever since.

In the early days, Princess Anne was not a fan. She does not have fond memories of her first experiences. 'At nineteen years old suddenly being dropped in the middle of the street, suddenly being told to pick someone and talk to them. Fun? No, I don't think so. A challenge.'

She has got used to the challenge over the years and likes to take her time talking to people at official engagements: 'If they have taken the time and trouble to come and see me, the very least I can do is to spend a few moments with them, and what's more it's something I thoroughly enjoy anyway.'

Kate obviously enjoys meeting the public and confessed, 'There's a real art to walkabouts. Everybody teases me in the family that I spend far too long chatting. I still have to … pick up a few more tips, I suppose.' When asked about the challenges facing her as a new member of the Royal Family, soon after her marriage to William, she admitted, 'It's obviously nerve-wracking, because I don't know the ropes really. William is obviously used to it, but I'm willing to learn quickly and work hard.'

Princess Anne thinks that the younger royals have taken things too far and become too touchy-feely, telling an interviewer, 'The theory was that you couldn't shake hands with everybody, so don't start. I kind of stick with that, but I've noticed others don't. It's become a shaking hands exercise rather than a walkabout.'

Interviewed by the BBC in 2011 on the eve of his ninetieth birthday, Prince Philip claimed, 'I reckon I've done my bit. I want to enjoy myself for a bit now. With less responsibility, less frantic rushing about, less preparation, less trying to think of something to say. On top of that, your memory's going. I can't remember names. Yes, I'm just sort of winding down.'

He finally stepped down and made his last solo public engagement on 2 August 2017 attending a Royal Marines Parade. Irreverent as ever, at a Buckingham Palace event following the announcement of his retirement, he told restaurateur, writer and broadcaster Prue Leith, 'I'm discovering what it's like to be on your last legs. But while you're still alive you might as well keep moving, or try to.'

Visiting Australia in October 2018 with Meghan at the start of their first official tour as a married couple, Prince Harry had an important announcement to make, 'We're both absolutely delighted to be here and really impressed to see you serving beer and tea in true Aussie style. We also genuinely couldn't think of a better place to announce, uh … the, uh … the upcoming baby. Boy or girl.'

CHAPTER 4

Causes and Credos

A longside their standard duties, there are certain causes that all members of the Royal Family hold dear. These include care for the environment and animal welfare, as well as children's charities and, more recently, mental health. Across the generations, the royals have taken a pioneering attitude towards issues, and have not been afraid to speak out and lead. The senior royals have set out a legacy that the next generation is keen to build upon.

During a tour of Nigeria in February 1956, the Queen and Prince Philip visited the Oji River leper settlement near Enugu. At the time, anyone suffering from leprosy was still treated as an outcast, even those who had been cured of the disease. The Queen listened to speeches and shook hands with former sufferers prompting journalist Barbara Ward to write, 'Qualities of grace and compassion shine through the spectacle of a young queen shaking hands with cured Nigerian lepers to reassure timid villagers who do not believe in the cure.'

Princess Margaret became President of the NSPCC in 1953 and was committed to the charity throughout her life. She also became a patron of the Terrence Higgins Trust, a British charity that campaigns and provides services related to HIV and sexual health, visiting regularly. After her death, David Wakefield from the charity said, 'As a public figure, she showed her support for a cause which is still unpopular today.'

Princess Diana prompted headlines and challenged widely held misconceptions about HIV/AIDS in 1987 when she opened the UK's first purpose-built HIV/AIDS unit at London's Middlesex Hospital. In the mid-eighties, the world was still terrified by the disease, largely because of a lack of understanding, and it was wrongly feared that it was passed on by touch. Diana shook the hand of a sufferer without wearing gloves.

♛

Princess Diana on caring – 'Anywhere I see suffering, that is where I want to be, doing what I can.' And, 'Every one of us needs to show how much we care for each other and, in the process, care for ourselves.'

♛

Diana was patron and president of a range of charities throughout her life, many of them focused on AIDS awareness, but also working on behalf of the homeless, children and the disabled while campaigning to ban the manufacture and use of landmines.

Green Matters

Prince Charles once asserted, 'I don't want my grandchildren or yours to come along and say to me, "Why the hell didn't you do something; you knew what the problem was."'

Care for the environment and a responsible attitude towards conservation and climate change are matters of grave importance to Charles. He warned, 'Like the sorcerer's apprentice causing havoc in his master's home when he couldn't control the spell which he had released, mankind runs a similar risk of laying waste his earthly home by thinking he's in control when he's clearly not.'

In the *Prince Charles at 70* television documentary that aired in 2018, William and Harry described how their father encouraged them to pick up litter. Harry explained, 'He took us litter picking when we were younger, on holiday … We thought this is perfectly normal, everyone must do it. We were there with our spikes, stabbing the rubbish into black plastic bags.' Harry was teased at school for his rubbish collecting but now, as a grown up, still does it automatically.

Charles explained, 'If we can stop the sky turning into a microwave oven, we still face the prospect of living in a garbage dump.' And, 'If you try to kick nature in the teeth and push her too far, she will kick you back.'

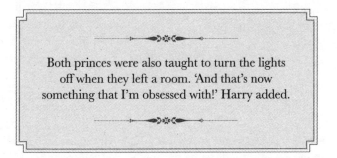

Both princes were also taught to turn the lights off when they left a room. 'And that's now something that I'm obsessed with!' Harry added.

Like Father Like Son

Although they are very different characters, Prince Charles and his father share many of the same concerns and interests. Philip has long been a committed environmentalist and has written a number of books on the subject. He was the first President of the World Wildlife Fund in the UK from its beginnings in 1961 until 1982, President of the WWF International from 1981 until 1996 and is now President Emeritus of the organization – renamed the World Wide Fund for Nature.

Interviewed by Fiona Bruce for the BBC to mark his ninetieth birthday in 2011, Philip explained his philosophy: 'If we've got this extraordinary diversity on this globe it seems awfully silly for us to destroy it. All these other creatures have an equal right to exist here, we have no more prior rights to the Earth than anybody else and if they're here let's give them a chance to survive.'

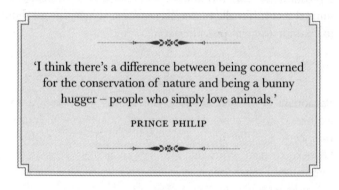

'I think there's a difference between being concerned for the conservation of nature and being a bunny hugger – people who simply love animals.'

PRINCE PHILIP

Warming to his theme, he felt that people who called themselves 'green' could sometimes be misguided and fail to see the real issues, 'People are more concerned about how you treat a donkey in Sicily than conservation.'

Philip is also the founder of the Alliance of Religions and Conservation, or ARC, which supports the work of religions around the world in protecting the environment. His ethos – 'If you believe in God … then you should feel a responsibility to care for his Creation.'

Philip's concern for conservation and animal welfare does not exclude being a keen shot and a vocal advocate of field sports. He observed, 'Fox hunting is a curious thing to ban because, of all the blood sports, it's the only one where the people following it don't come anywhere near a wild animal at all.'

He has also compared field sports such as hunting, shooting and fishing to a butcher's work, so managing to offend fairly comprehensively. 'I don't think doing it [butchering animals to sell as meat] for money makes it any more moral. I don't think a prostitute is more moral than a wife, but they are doing the same thing. It is really rather like saying it is perfectly all right to commit adultery providing you don't enjoy it.'

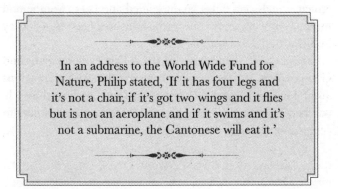

Passionate in his beliefs, Philip has ruffled more than a few feathers over the years. He condemned poachers who hunted rhinoceros for their horns, a popular ingredient in traditional Chinese medicine. Speaking in New York in 1962, he said, 'For some incomprehensible reason, they seem to think it acts as an aphrodisiac. They might as well grind up chair legs.'

> In an address to the World Wide Fund for Nature, Philip stated, 'If it has four legs and it's not a chair, if it's got two wings and it flies but is not an aeroplane and if it swims and it's not a submarine, the Cantonese will eat it.'

Although happy to accept an award for conservation in Thailand in 1991, this did not stop Philip from criticizing the host country in his speech: 'Your country is one of the most notorious centres of trading in endangered species in the world.'

Dogs and Cats

Along with their affection for animals in general, the Royal Family tend to be dog people. The Queen is famous for her iconic Pembroke Welsh corgis and more latterly dorgis – a crossbreed created when one of Princess Margaret's dachshunds mated with one of the Queen's corgis. Prince Philip and Prince Edward generally prefer labradors or spaniels, nicknamed 'the Hoovers' by the family. Princess Anne's favoured English bull terriers gained an unfortunate reputation for biting, while Prince Andrew and his daughters usually go for Norfolk terriers. The Duchess of Cornwall is known to be a fan of Jack Russells – 'They are such intelligent dogs' – and she and Charles adopted two, Bluebell and Beth, from Battersea Dogs and Cats Home in 2012. William and Kate have a black cocker spaniel, Lupo, a present from Kate's mother, while Meghan and Harry have Meghan's beagle Guy and a labrador retriever.

This affection for dogs and pets is reflected in the pet graveyard set in a quiet corner of the Sandringham estate. The Queen's beloved first corgi, Susan, from whom all her others were descended, was buried there in 1959 with the simple inscription on her gravestone, 'The faithful companion of the Queen'. The majority of Susan's descendants are also there, although Monty, who famously starred alongside his royal mistress in the James Bond sketch for the opening ceremony of the 2012 Olympics, is buried near Queen Victoria's collie, Noble, at Balmoral where he died.

Many of the graves carry simple, affectionate epitaphs while some reflect the dog's character. Sandringham Fern, a roan cocker spaniel, is described as a 'tireless worker and mischievous character', while the black labrador Sandringham Brae is called 'a gentleman amongst dogs'. The cemetery wall is set with plaques commemorating other royal pets, though no cats. The Queen is reportedly allergic to them, and one of the few royals to prefer cats to dogs is Princess Michael of Kent who is very attached to her Siamese and Burmese pets.

Prince Philip is a keen birdwatcher and was patron of the British Trust for Ornithology from 1987 until his retirement. He has made his opinion of cats very clear over the years. Visiting a project for the protection of turtle doves in Anguilla in 1965 he suggested, 'Cats kill far more birds than men. Why don't you have a slogan: "Kill a cat and save a bird"?'

Forty years later, his views had not shifted: 'People don't like to admit it but cats catch an enormous number of small wild birds. But people are very attached to their cats – it's a fact of life.'

The Outspoken Prince

In addition to his efforts to raise awareness of the dangers of climate change and champion organic farming long before such concerns became mainstream, Prince Charles is known for his interest in alternative medicine and holistic treatments, including homeopathy. This has created a somewhat eccentric public image, which he long ago came to terms with. He explained:

> I can only go muddling along pursuing the sort of things I think are right and true, and hope there's a result. I'm not somebody overburdened with a sense of self-confidence about such things. I always feel that I should be somewhat reticent, otherwise you end up thinking you are more important than you are. I just go on trying to encourage, to help. And he also said:
> I'm not interested in the occult or any of these things. I'm purely interested in being open-minded. As soon as the word "holistic" is out of my mouth, I am aware that many people are overcome by a desire to tiptoe to the door and head to the bar to recover.

Charles thought his position as Prince of Wales gave him a useful opportunity to speak out: 'People come [to hear me] out of curiosity if nothing else.'

Charles is passionate about organic farming but quickly realized that 'One of the great difficulties of converting to organic farming turned out to be convincing others that you had not taken complete leave of your senses.'

He converted 900 acres of the Duchy Home Farm estate at Highgrove to organic farming in 1986 and is now credited as a pioneer, but at the time was criticized and accused of merely trying to avoid modern farming techniques. His farm increasingly uses biodynamic methods because 'in farming, as in gardening, I happen to believe that if you treat the land with love and respect (in particular, respect for the idea that it has an almost living soul, bound up in the mysterious, everlasting cycles of nature) then it will repay you in kind.'

When William and Kate visited Cumbria in June 2019, they chatted to farmers about the challenges facing modern farming. They also had the opportunity to try their hand at sheep-shearing at Deepdale Hall Farm. After helping farmer Jack Cartmel with one sheep, William stood back to admire his handy work. 'She's not going to be happy with her haircut!' he joked.

Prince Charles is well aware of his reputation for talking to his plants and, when asked about his gardens at Highgrove, replied, 'I just come to talk to the plants really. It's very important to talk – they respond, don't they?' And, in the same vein, 'To get the best results, you must talk to your vegetables.'

Princess Diana once commented sceptically on Charles's passion for gardening: 'He loves his garden, but as soon as he's finished sorting out every inch of it he will get bored with it and take up something else. He's like that.'

On another occasion he said, 'Only the other day I was inquiring of an entire bed of old-fashioned roses, forced to listen to my ramblings on the meaning of the universe as I sat cross-legged in the lotus position in front of them.'

'Here I am robed, sandalled, shaven-headed and with a rather faraway look in my eyes,' the Prince once described himself, with more than a touch of irony. He has also admitted, 'My sense of humour will get me into trouble one day.'

All this, however, can't disguise how hard he has worked at Highgrove: 'I have also put my back into [my gardens], and as a result have probably rendered myself prematurely decrepit in the process.'

Modern Architecture

Famously critical of some modern architecture, one of Prince Charles's most memorable quotes referred to the plans for an extension to the National Gallery in Trafalgar Square in May 1984. He said, 'It is like a kind of vast municipal fire station … What is proposed is like a monstrous carbuncle on the face of a much-loved and elegant friend.' He was speaking at the 150th anniversary of the Royal Institute of British Architects at Hampton Court Palace and he definitely stirred things up.

He had been expected to make a short speech, raise a glass of champagne and present the Royal Gold Medal for Architecture to architect Charles Correa. Instead, he criticized almost every aspect of RIBA's approach and trashed the proposed National Gallery design. His words caused such a furore that the carbuncle was never constructed. Instead of Ahrends, Burton and Koralek's planned extension, a post-modern design by Robert Venturi and Denise Scott Brown was built instead.

Charles is also on record saying, 'You have to give this much to the Luftwaffe: when it knocked down our buildings it did not replace them with anything more offensive than rubble. We did that.'

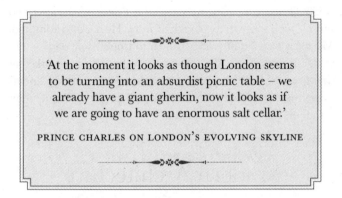

'At the moment it looks as though London seems to be turning into an absurdist picnic table – we already have a giant gherkin, now it looks as if we are going to have an enormous salt cellar.'

PRINCE CHARLES ON LONDON'S EVOLVING SKYLINE

The Hardest Working Royal

When statistics are compiled, Princess Anne regularly tops the list as the hardest working member of 'The Firm'. She is the patron of over two hundred organizations and has been President of Save the Children since 1970 and patron since 2016. She spends a considerable amount of time visiting the charity's projects both at home and overseas.

Speaking about her work with Save the Children, Anne said, 'The fund offered me the chance of a Presidency with a working life, a chance to do more.' She added, 'As President … one of the few things I suppose I can achieve is publicity.' Furthermore, 'I decided right from the start that if I was going to become involved with an organization, I was going to try and do something for them, apart from just lending my name.' And, crucially, 'If you don't invest in people at the earliest point of their lives you miss an opportunity – and you never get the chance again.'

Talking about her trip to Africa for the charity in 1982, Anne said, '"Wasn't it very depressing?" people ask. No. It was very encouraging – you're doing something constructive and you're doing it in the right sort of way.'

Beliefs and Causes

Four nifty quotes from Prince William... First, 'I'm reasonably headstrong about what I believe in, and what I go for, and I've got fantastic people around me who give me great support and advice.' Also, 'I think it's very important that you make your own decision about what you are. Therefore you're responsible for your actions, so you don't blame other people.'

On independence – 'I am as independent as I want to be, same as Catherine and Harry. We've all grown up differently to other generations and I very much feel that if I can do it myself, I want to do it myself.' And self-deprecatingly, 'I'm always open for people saying I'm wrong because most of the time I am.'

In winter 2009, William spent a cold night 'sleeping rough' with homeless teenagers near Blackfriar's Bridge in London. The event was part of an initiative organized by Centrepoint, the homeless charity of which Princess Diana had been a patron. The idea had been to highlight how poverty, mental illness and substance abuse all contribute to problems of homelessness. Afterwards, William said, 'These kinds of events are much more fulfilling to me than dressing up in a suit.'

Diana's ethos and strong feelings about charity work have had a lasting impact on her two sons. William echoed her words when he claimed, 'My guiding principles in life are to be honest, genuine, thoughtful and caring.' Also, 'People say it's not ambitious, but it is actually quite ambitious wanting to help people.'

Prince Harry on the death of Diana, when he was very young:

I didn't want to be in the position I was in, but I eventually pulled my head out of the sand, started listening to people, and decided to use my role for good. I am now fired up and energized and love charity stuff, meeting people and making them laugh.

Losing your mother at such a young age does end up shaping your life massively, of course it does. And now I find myself trying to be there and give advice to other people who are in similar positions.

I never really dealt with what had actually happened. So there was a lot of buried emotion, and I still didn't even want to think about it.

I really regret not talking about it. It is okay to suffer, but as long as you talk about it. It is not a weakness. Weakness is having a problem and not recognizing it and not solving that problem.

Every day, depending on what I'm doing, I wonder

what it would be like if she was here, and what she would say, and how she would be making everybody else laugh. Who knows what the situation would be, what the world would be like, if she were still around.

Speaking about the media's tendency to make comparisons between Princess Diana and her daughters-in-law, William was clear. The Cambridges and Sussexes may wish to continue Diana's work, but they are their own people and will do it in their own way. Furthermore, 'There's no pressure; it is about carving your own future. No one is going to try to fill my mother's shoes. What she did was fantastic. It's about making your own future and your own destiny, and Kate will do a very good job of that.'

Initially, Kate struggled speaking in public – 'I find doing speeches nerve-wracking.' But she, like William, Harry and Meghan, was committed to improving the welfare of children worldwide and changing attitudes towards mental health. 'I really hope I can make a difference, even in the smallest way. I am looking forward to helping as much as I can.'

Prince Harry is known for his support of children's, mental health, military and sporting charities, while Meghan has been standing up to gender inequality since the age of eleven when she wrote a letter to Hillary Clinton on the subject, and she has since worked with the UN and as a global ambassador for World Vision. Both are keen champions of women and girl's rights and education, wanting to use their position to make a positive difference in the world.

Together with the news of the couple's engagement, it was also announced that Meghan would stop acting to concentrate on charitable work. She told the BBC, 'What's been really exciting, as we talk about this as the transition out of my career … is that the causes that have been very important to me, I can focus even more energy on.'

"I've never wanted to be a lady who lunches – I've always wanted to be a woman who works. And this type of [charity] work is what feeds my soul and fuels my purpose.'

MEGHAN MARKLE

'Conversations with my mother, father, my grandparents, as I've grown up have obviously driven me towards wanting to try and make a difference as much as possible.'

PRINCE HARRY

In the past, Meghan said, 'If things are wrong and there is a lack of justice, and there is an inequality, then someone needs to say something.' This echoes Harry's view that 'part of my role and part of my job is to shine a spotlight on issues that need that spotlight, whether it's people, whether it's causes, issues, whatever it is.'

He wants to build on Princess Diana's legacy: 'It's something my mother believed in. If you are in a position of privilege you can put your name to something that you genuinely believe in, you can smash any stigma you want, and you can encourage anybody to do anything.'

Visiting the Girls Summit in Kathmandu in 2016, Harry spoke eloquently about the need for girls to have equal access to education: 'While the unique challenges faced by girls is not a topic I have spoken much about in the past, I think it's important to acknowledge … there are way too many obstacles between girls and the opportunities they deserve. I believe it is vitally important for men like me to acknowledge this as loudly and openly as role models do.'

He's clearly on the same wavelength as Meghan. Speaking in October 2018 at an event to celebrate the 125th anniversary of women's suffrage in New Zealand, the first country to give women the vote in 1893, she said:

> Women's suffrage is about feminism, but feminism is about fairness. Suffrage is not simply about the right to vote but also about what that represents: the basic and fundamental human right of being able to participate in the choices for your future and that of your community, the involvement and voice that allows you to be a part of the very world that you are a part of.

Harry has also supported HeForShe, the campaign for gender equality: 'This is not just about women, we men need to recognize the part we play, too. Real men treat women with dignity and give them the respect they deserve.' Meghan added that women 'don't need to find a voice', but they need encouragement to use it.

Interviewed by *Elle* magazine in 2015 before she met the Prince, Meghan talked about her experiences as a biracial woman: 'I have come to embrace that. To say who I am, to share where I'm from, to voice my pride in being a strong, confident mixed-race woman.'

Prince William spoke out in June 2019 – when opening a new London centre for the Albert Kennedy Trust, a charity that helps homeless LGBT young people – saying that it would be 'absolutely fine by me' if one of his own children identified as LGBT. 'I'd fully support whatever decisions they make. It worries me how many barriers, persecution and hate they'd face. But that's for all of us to try and correct.'

He added, 'I think communication is so important with everything. In order to help understand it you've got to talk a lot about stuff and make sure how to support each other and how to go through the process.'

Having famously appeared as herself in the Bond sketch at the opening of the 2012 Olympic Games in London, the Queen agreed to take part in another film, this time to publicise the Invictus Games in 2016.

The Invictus Games Foundation was launched by Harry in 2014 as an international sporting event for injured military personnel and veterans. The cause is close to Harry's heart and his grandmother was happy to help. In the skit, President Barack and Michelle Obama are sharing fighting talk about the Games. The smiling Queen looks totally unconvinced and dismissively says, 'Oh, really! Please!'

Harry commented that the scene took just a few minutes to film: 'She's the Queen, she's busy … She's so incredibly skilled, she only needs one take.' He thought his grandmother had thoroughly enjoyed her role, adding, 'You could see that look on her face, at the age of ninety, thinking, "Why the hell does nobody ask me to do these things more often?"'

CHAPTER 5

Being Royal

eing royal in the UK is very much a family affair, with every member having a role to play. They are rarely off-duty. 'Monarchy involves the whole family, which means that different age groups are part of it. There are people who can look, for instance, at the Queen Mother and identify with that generation, or with us, or with our children,' Prince Philip observed.

In the early days of World War II during the Blitz, when London and other cities were being bombed daily, it was suggested that the Royal Family should be evacuated to Canada for their safety. The Queen Mother refused categorically: 'The princesses would never leave without me – and I could not leave without the King – and of course, the King will never leave.'

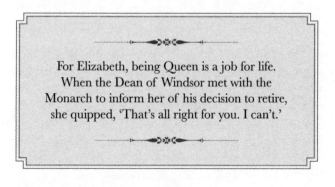

For Elizabeth, being Queen is a job for life.
When the Dean of Windsor met with the
Monarch to inform her of his decision to retire,
she quipped, 'That's all right for you. I can't.'

The monarchy may have modernized during the Queen's reign but some things never change. Queen Mary, the wife of King George V who reigned from 1910 to 1936, had the following advice for her young granddaughter Elizabeth: 'You are a member of the British Royal Family. We are never tired, and we all love hospitals.' She also passed on a couple of very practical suggestions: 'During public engagements one should sit down whenever possible and avail oneself of toilet facilities whenever the opportunity arises.'

Prince Philip put it far more bluntly when asked for his secret to coping with visits and public appearances: 'I never pass up a chance to go to the loo or take a poo.'

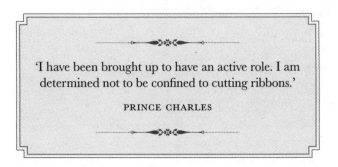

'I have been brought up to have an active role. I am determined not to be confined to cutting ribbons.'

PRINCE CHARLES

And Princess Anne? 'If you stop having nerves, you're not doing the job as well as you should.' She's also on record saying, 'Survival: that's the name of the game.' When asked about preparation for life as a royal, Prince Charles said, 'You pick it up as you go along. You watch and learn … I learned the way a monkey learns – by watching its parents.' And Zara Phillips clarified: 'The senior members of the Royal Family work very hard and I don't think people quite realize that.'

When Prince Edward married Sophie Rhys-Jones in 1999, the Queen teased her new daughter-in-law that she was 'the perfect royal'. She joked that the magic formula to be a successful member of 'The Firm' was to have the warmth of Fergie, the steadfastness of Mark 'Foggy' Phillips and the poise of Princess Michael of Kent.

Growing up Royal

When asked about what it was like to be a member of the Royal Family, Prince Edward said:

> There's a certain amount of acting involved. If you played the part of a member of the Royal Family as a down-to-earth character it probably wouldn't work … I may be a human being but I certainly wouldn't describe myself as normal. And that can never be the case. I mean if you have ever followed me down the street you notice people turn and always do a double take – and then again I am always accompanied by a policeman.

Princess Anne has a slightly different take: 'The idea of opting out is a non-starter.' She continued, 'I am the Queen's daughter, and as a daughter I get less involved than the boys. I doubt if the next generation will be involved at all.'

'I never was a fairy tale princess …
I never was and I never will be.'

PRINCESS ANNE ON HER PUBLIC IMAGE

Anne was also always clear on her position in the order of succession, 'I've always accepted the role of being second in everything from quite an early age. You adopt that position as part of your experience. You start off in life very much a tail-end Charlie, at the back of the line.'

Princess Margaret understood the sense of feeling less important only too well. The Queen's younger sister described herself growing up as 'the heir presumptive to the heir apparent'. She formed a close bond with her niece, but felt Anne was far better equipped to deal with her position in life: 'Anne's more positive than I was. She's much tougher, too. She's been brought up in a different atmosphere.'

Like her aunt, Anne had married and divorced a commoner, was independent, prone to speaking her mind and didn't suffer fools gladly. When she was young, Margaret gave her advice on public appearances and what to wear.

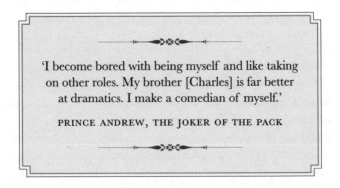

'I become bored with being myself and like taking on other roles. My brother [Charles] is far better at dramatics. I make a comedian of myself.'

PRINCE ANDREW, THE JOKER OF THE PACK

Anne was aware that her public image was not always very positive, explaining, 'When you're a youngster practically everything you do is wrong in terms of your ability to fit in with people. You don't know what you want to do in life.' Charles's position was slightly different, being the heir to the throne. 'I didn't suddenly wake up in my pram one day and say "Yippee!" It just dawns on you slowly that people are interested … and slowly you get the idea that you have a certain duty and responsibility. It's better that way, rather than someone suddenly telling you "You must do this" and "You must do that", because of who you are. It's one of those things you grow up in.'

As one of the younger generation of royals, Harry was aware of how his position could mark him out as different and he wanted to be valued for himself: 'I don't want to be liked by someone just because of who I am. You know, I don't want the sycophantic … people hanging around.'

Speaking about friends, William said, 'I don't deliberately select my friends because of their background. If I enjoy someone's company, then that's all that counts. I have many different friends who aren't from the same background as me and we get on really well.'

Being a member of the Royal Family might bring amazing advantages and privileges that few could dream of, but Prince Philip has always been clear that there are also very obvious downsides: 'We live in what virtually amounts to a museum, which does not happen to a lot of people.' Perhaps hankering for a simple life, he mused, 'I never see any home cooking – all I get is fancy stuff.'

When they were small children, Prince Charles commented on his two young sons, 'They are normal little boys, who are unlucky enough to create an abnormal amount of attention.' Diana added, 'They're little minxes' but 'I have to watch what I say in front of Prince William. He's so quick on the uptake that he copies everything.' And that of the two, 'Harry is the mischievous one.'

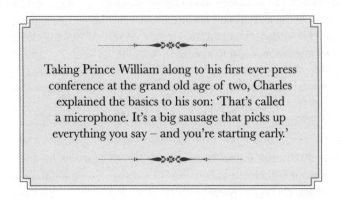

Taking Prince William along to his first ever press conference at the grand old age of two, Charles explained the basics to his son: 'That's called a microphone. It's a big sausage that picks up everything you say – and you're starting early.'

'William is the greatest possible fun. He's a most enjoyable child, but then one always thinks one's own child is,' Charles once commented, although he later said, 'He's getting angrier and noisier by the day.' And William could certainly let rip. After he had been introduced to Bob Geldof when the Live Aid campaigner met Charles to discuss global poverty and famine, he cast a critical eye over Geldof and asked his father loudly, 'Why do you talk to that man? He's all dirty. He's got scruffy hair and wet shoes.' Charles clearly took a different view: 'I wish I had been born Bob Geldof.'

When a classmate at Wetherby School in Kensington asked William which prep school he'd be going to, William replied, 'I don't know. I'm not allowed to know 'cos of security.' He also had the ultimate putdown for a fellow pupil at his nursery school: 'My daddy is the Prince of Wales and he can beat up your daddy.' Daddy might not have approved.

Asked about growing up as one of the Royal Family, Harry reckoned, 'To be honest, dinner conversations was the worst bit about being a child and listening to the boring people around me.' He added, 'You can imagine the kind of dinner parties I had to go to at a young age ... pretty dull.'

School Days

Prince Charles found his own school days challenging. He started at Hill House in London as a day boy but then boarded at Cheam School in Surrey from September 1958. When writing his first letter home he asked sadly, 'I know my mother is the Queen, but how do I put that on the envelope?'

He immediately disliked the fact that his position made him different from the other pupils and felt embarrassed by the attention. Everyone at school heard the Queen's announcement from the stadium in Cardiff that she was making him Prince of Wales. 'I remember being acutely embarrassed when it was announced. I heard this marvellous great cheer ... [from the crowd] ... and I think for a little boy of nine it was rather bewildering. All the others turned and looked at me in amazement.'

If Charles found his prep school hard, Gordonstoun in North East Scotland was in a different league. This was his father's old school and Philip had loved his time there. The school had a reputation for toughness and Charles once described it as 'Colditz in kilts', and 'A prison of privilege'.

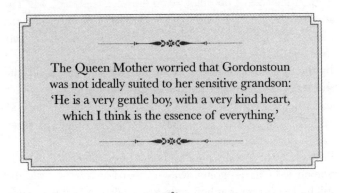

The Queen Mother worried that Gordonstoun was not ideally suited to her sensitive grandson: 'He is a very gentle boy, with a very kind heart, which I think is the essence of everything.'

Philip's views on education were fixed by his own experience: 'Children may be indulged at home, but school is expected to be a Spartan and disciplined experience in the process of developing into self-controlled, considerate and independent adults.'

However, Charles struggled and was never happy at Gordonstoun, although speaking in 1975 he acknowledged its benefits:

I did not enjoy school as much as I might have, but this was because I am happier at home than anywhere else ... I had this schoolboy dream that I was going to escape and hide in the forest, in a place where no one could find me, so that I wouldn't have to go back to school.

I hated that institution, just as I hated leaving home. When you lead a perfectly agreeable existence you don't want to go back to cold showers at seven in the morning and a quick run before breakfast ... But Gordonstoun developed my will power and self control, helped me to discipline myself, and I think that discipline, not in the sense of making you bath in cold water, but in the Latin sense – giving shape and form and tidiness to your life – is the most important thing your education can do.'

By the time Andrew attended, the regime had softened – the showers were no longer icy and girls were admitted.

Princess Anne loved school and could never wait to go back. She envied Charles going away to boarding school while she still had a governess at home, and was delighted when she was finally allowed to go to the all-girls boarding school Benenden in Kent when she was thirteen. Her first impressions were: 'Continuous noise and the fact that everywhere you turned there were so many people,' and 'Noise and smells – that's what school meant to me – cabbage and polish.'

She quickly got the measure of her classmates and appreciated their brutal honesty, describing them as 'a caustic lot who knew exactly what they thought about other people and saved one a lot of embarrassment'.

Like Charles, Anne was keen to fit in and did not like the extra attention her background brought. She quickly realized that humour was a very useful weapon. During riding lessons she would make her horse buck to amuse her friends, and when collected from school to attend a private lunch with the Archbishop of Canterbury she joked, 'Watch my halo!' before anyone else had the chance to tease her about it.

Prince Charles did not want a repetition of his own miserable schooldays for his sons. William and Harry were the first royals to go to nursery school, at Mrs Mynor's, just a stone's throw from their Kensington Palace home. On William's first day at the pre-preparatory Wetherby School in London, he was greeted by a posse of press and photographers. He imagined they would be there again when he arrived on day two. 'Where have all the photographers gone?' he asked, earning a gentle reprimand from Diana, 'Don't be so grand, William.'

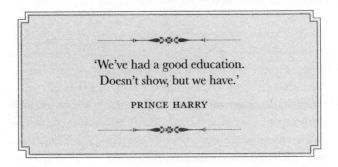

'We've had a good education.
Doesn't show, but we have.'

PRINCE HARRY

Like their father, both William and Harry went to boarding school from the age of eight but they attended Ludgrove School in Berkshire where pupils built dens and camps, and were encouraged to grow their own vegetables and flowers in the school gardens. They then followed their mother's father and brother to Eton where they were a short walk from the family home at Windsor Castle.

Speaking about his lack of artistic talent, Prince William admitted, 'Harry can paint but I can't. He has our father's talent while I, on the other hand, am about the biggest idiot on a piece of canvas. I did do a couple of drawings at Eton, which were put on display. Teachers thought they were examples of modern art, but in fact I was just trying to paint a house!'

It's not yet known where the next generation will go to school. Prince George started at Thomas's Battersea at the age of four, in 2017, with Princess Charlotte following two years later. They could remain there as day pupils until the age of thirteen.

University

Prince Charles went to Trinity College, Cambridge, in 1966 and also spent a term at Aberystwyth University studying the Welsh language and history. Of his university days Charles said it had been 'marvellous to have three years when you are not bound by anything, and not married, and haven't got any particular job'.

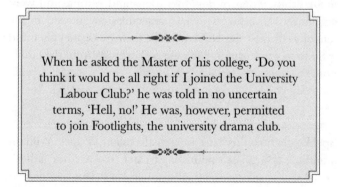

When he asked the Master of his college, 'Do you think it would be all right if I joined the University Labour Club?' he was told in no uncertain terms, 'Hell, no!' He was, however, permitted to join Footlights, the university drama club.

Charles began by reading anthropology, archaeology and history at Trinity but partway through his degree switched to the British constitution 'because I'm probably going to be King'.

During Charles's time at Cambridge, the strict curfew governing the hour at which the college gates were closed each night was relaxed. The Prince rather regretted this, commenting, 'It was a great challenge to climb over the wall. Half the fun of university life is breaking the rules.'

Prince William decided to break with the traditional Oxbridge route followed by his father and other members of the Royal Family. Instead, he opted for St Andrews in Scotland, where he began a degree in art history, later swapping to geography. 'I just want to go to university and have fun – I want to be an ordinary student … It's not like I'm getting married – though that's what it feels like sometimes.' But he reckoned, 'My father thinks I'm the laziest person on earth.'

Andrew Neil, who was then Lord Rector of the university, recalled, 'His main concern was the size of the swimming pool because he was into water polo at the time.' He added, 'I informed him that St Andrews was full of beautiful and very bright young women and I'm sure that's what clinched it.' The decision worked out well for William when he met his future wife there while sharing student accommodation.

Looking back, he said, 'I don't like being treated differently from anybody else,' while a fellow student commented, 'He was just one of the lads.' William added, 'I do think I'm a country boy at heart. I love the buzz of towns and going out with friends and sitting with them drinking and whatever – it's fun. But, at the same time, I like space and freedom.'

Prince Philip has been awarded a vast number of honorary degrees, titles and chancellorships over the years. His first degree was a Doctorate of Law from the University of Wales in 1949. Awarded a Doctorate of Science by Reading University in 1957, he commented, 'It must be pretty well known that I never earned an honest degree in my life and I certainly never made any effort to gain an honorary one.'

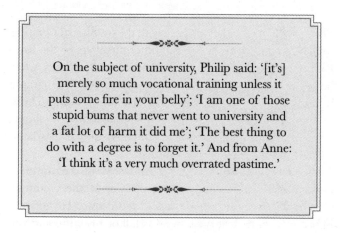

On the subject of university, Philip said: '[it's] merely so much vocational training unless it puts some fire in your belly'; 'I am one of those stupid bums that never went to university and a fat lot of harm it did me'; 'The best thing to do with a degree is to forget it.' And from Anne: 'I think it's a very much overrated pastime.'

Accepting an award in 1960 after a glowing introduction, Philip said, 'Some people might well feel that your Vice-Chancellor has succeeded in presenting me for this honorary degree, not just in a good light, but in a positively rosy glow of perfection. I can only imagine that he has taken Disraeli's advice that, "Everyone likes flattery, and when you come to royalty you should lay it on with a trowel."'

Serving Queen and Country

After graduating, Charles joined the RAF as a Flight Lieutenant in March 1971 and then a few months later joined the Royal Navy as Acting Sub-Lieutenant. He served until 1976 by which time he had been promoted to Wing Commander in the RAF and Commander in the Navy. He explained his decision to sign up:

> It is pointless and ill-informed to say that I am entering a profession trained in killing. The Services in the first place are there for fast, efficient and well-trained action in defence. Surely the Services must attract a large number of duty-conscious people? Otherwise who else would subject themselves to being square-bashed, shouted at by petty officers and made to do ghastly things in Force Ten gales? I am entering the RAF and then the Navy because I believe I can contribute something to this county by so doing. To me it is a worthwhile occupation, and one which I am convinced will stand me in good stead for the rest of my life.

And looking back? 'It's given me a marvellous opportunity to get as close to the "ordinary" British chap as possible.' Though Charles did once threaten some of those 'ordinary chaps' who were trying to de-bag him with an archaic royal punishment: 'I can send you to the Tower you know. It's quite within my power.'

When asked about his life as a member of 'The Firm' in 1992, Prince Philip answered, 'I'd much rather have stayed in the Navy, frankly.' Questioned about how hard it had been for him to give up a very promising career as a naval officer, he replied, 'Well, how long is a piece of string?'

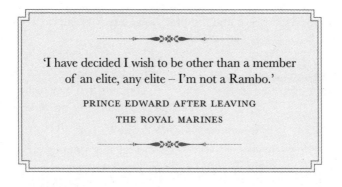

'I have decided I wish to be other than a member
of an elite, any elite – I'm not a Rambo.'

PRINCE EDWARD AFTER LEAVING
THE ROYAL MARINES

William and Harry relished their time in the armed forces. Harry
went to Sandhurst in May 2005 as William was completing his
degree at St Andrews. William joked that his brother was 'going
as a guinea pig first to see what happens.'

William also emphasized that 'The last thing I want to do
is be mollycoddled or wrapped up in cotton wool because if
I was to join the army, I'd want to go where my men went and
I'd want to do what they did.' Harry agreed: 'There is no way I
am going to put myself through Sandhurst and then sit on my
arse back home while my boys are out fighting for their country.'

Harry later reflected on his time in Afghanistan in 2007 to
2008: 'It's very nice to be a sort of normal person for once;
I think it's about as normal as I'm going to get.' He also
appreciated the camaraderie away from the glare of publicity
and pressures of royal life: 'It's good fun to be with just a
normal bunch of guys, listening to their problems, listening to
what they think.'

And did he miss it? 'Personally, as I said, I want to serve my
country. I've done it once, and I'm still in the army, I feel as
though I should get the opportunity to do it again.' Moreover,
'Anyone who says they don't enjoy the army is mad – you can
spend a week hating it and the next week it could be the best

thing in the world and the best job you could ever, ever wish for. It has got so much to offer.'

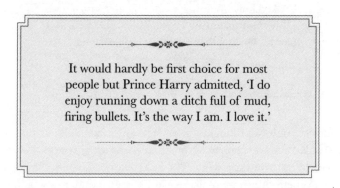

It would hardly be first choice for most people but Prince Harry admitted, 'I do enjoy running down a ditch full of mud, firing bullets. It's the way I am. I love it.'

Harry spent ten years in the army, rising to the rank of Captain and completing two tours of Afghanistan. On the sort of treatment he had received he explained, 'Everyone is really well looked after here by the Gurkhas, the food is fantastic – goat curries, chicken curries – probably shouldn't say goat curries, but yeah, it's really good fun and, yeah, we're really well looked after.'

Prince William followed his brother to Sandhurst in 2006 as an officer cadet and then transferred to RAF College Cranwell to train as a pilot, going on to complete RAF search and rescue helicopter training in early 2009, achieving the rank of Flight Lieutenant.

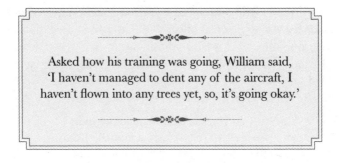

Asked how his training was going, William said, 'I haven't managed to dent any of the aircraft, I haven't flown into any trees yet, so, it's going okay.'

Prince Andrew's thoughts on his nephew Prince William joining the RAF were straightforward: 'The simple piece of advice would be "you should have joined the Navy".'

When questioned about his future in 2013, William answered, 'I'm still trying to decide. It's a really difficult one because I really enjoy my time in the Air Force. And I'd love to continue it. But the pressures of my other life are building. And fighting them off or balancing the two of them has proven quite difficult.' He left the RAF in September 2013 and then trained for his civil pilot's licence, spending just over two years working for the East Anglian Air Ambulance.

The Reality of Royalty

Prince Charles once jokingly described the monarchy as 'the oldest profession in the world'. He also said, 'Were it not for my ability to see the funny side of my life, I would have been committed to an institution long ago.' And, he added ruefully, 'All the time I feel I must justify my existence.'

Diana echoed his views: 'Being a princess isn't all it's cracked up to be.' And when asked about her role as a member of the

Royal Family with official duties, she added, 'Thirty per cent fantastic, seventy per cent sheer slog.' Later, she noted, 'I knew what my job was; it was to go out and meet the people and love them.' But life as a royal had some perks, not least the freedom from having to deal with everyday trivia. As she once stated, 'I don't even know how to use a parking meter, let alone a phone box.'

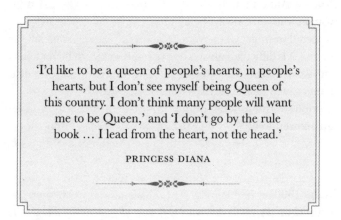

'I'd like to be a queen of people's hearts, in people's hearts, but I don't see myself being Queen of this country. I don't think many people will want me to be Queen,' and 'I don't go by the rule book … I lead from the heart, not the head.'

PRINCESS DIANA

Speaking about official royal engagements, Diana suggested, 'Imagine having to go to a wedding every day of your life – as the bride – well, that's a bit what it's like.' Furthermore, 'Although you are tired you just have to get on with the job.' And on a practical problem, 'The trouble with being a princess is that it is so hard to have a pee.' But not all doom and gloom. Diana's first solo overseas tour was to Norway in February 1984 and Prince Charles sent her a note saying, 'We were so proud of you,' from 'Willie Wombat and I'.

Speaking about his mother as Sovereign, Prince Andrew thought, 'It's slightly complicated for people to grasp the idea of a head of state in human form.' The Queen was clear, 'I have to be seen to be believed.'

Princess Anne thought there was more pressure on the royal women who were always being judged on their appearance and expected to smile, whenever, whatever. 'You can't smile all the time … it is difficult, I always think, to take an intelligent interest and wear a grin. Male members of royalty are not expected to meet such high standards and can appear serious or distant in public without being criticized. Men can be serious. They are allowed to be.'

In the 1990s, when a great deal of press and public attention focused on Princess Diana, and the Queen Mother as she approached her hundredth year, the Queen sighed to a member of staff: 'My mother's a star. My daughter-in-law's a star. Where does that leave me?'

Charles has the dubious distinction of being the oldest as well as the longest-serving heir to the throne in British history, so he has had a long time to consider his role. He has spoken on the subject many times, once saying, 'There is no set-out role for me. It depends entirely what I make of it … I'm really rather an awkward problem.'

Reflecting on the traditional motto of the Prince

of Wales – *Ich Dien* meaning 'I serve' – Charles reflected, '"I serve" is a marvellous motto to have. If you have a sense of duty, and I like to think I have, then service is something that you give to people, particularly if they want you – but sometimes if they don't.' He has also said, 'I am used to being regarded as an anachronism. In fact, I am coming round to think it is rather grand.'

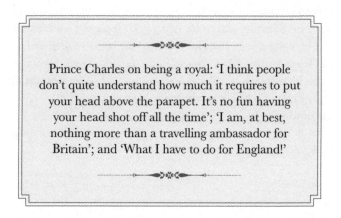

Prince Charles on being a royal: 'I think people don't quite understand how much it requires to put your head above the parapet. It's no fun having your head shot off all the time'; 'I am, at best, nothing more than a travelling ambassador for Britain'; and 'What I have to do for England!'

Charles has also commented on the predictability that is part of his role: 'You can't understand what it's like to have your whole life mapped out for you a year in advance. It's so awful to be programmed. I know what I'll be doing next week, next month, even next year. At times I get so fed up with the whole idea.' No wonder then that he has also said, 'I like to stir things up, to throw a proverbial royal brick through the plate glass of pompous professional pride and jump feet first into the kind of spaghetti bolognaise which clogs this country from one end to the other.'

Charles is well aware of his reputation for speaking his mind, though, and that voicing his opinions could get him into trouble, reflecting, 'I have come to the conclusion that basically I ought to keep my mouth shut during any election campaign.'

On his wife's sudden succession to the throne in 1952, Prince Philip explained, 'There were plenty of people telling me what not to do.' However, positive guidance was in short supply. 'I had to try to support the Queen as best I could without getting in the way. The difficulty was to find things that might be useful.'

There were no rules or job description, no precedent for him to follow and he had to work out his role for himself. Speaking to the British-based American press at a lunch at the end of 2000, Philip said, 'I'm, I suppose, a pragmatist. I mean, I'm here, and I might as well get on with it. There's no good saying "what if" all the time. You can't go round all your life envying other people or wishing you were doing something else.'

Princess Margaret famously said, 'I have always had a dread of becoming a passenger in life' and that 'I have as much privacy as a goldfish in a bowl.'

Taking up the theme, Prince Andrew elaborated, 'If you live in that goldfish bowl and you are a public figure, then to a certain extent you've got to expect somebody to throw a stone and you've got to live with it.' Also, 'People say to me: "Would you like to swap your life with me for twenty-four hours? Your life must be very strange." But of course, I have not experienced any other life. It's not strange to me.'

Heard about Prince Edward and *It's a Royal Knockout*? Having managed to persuade some of his family members to reluctantly join him in a TV game show in June 1987, he explained, 'It's an experiment, a very radical venture.' The Queen was said to be highly dubious about the idea, and Philip felt their children's participation was 'unwise and unwelcome'. Four teams led by Edward, Anne, Andrew and Sarah competed, with the proceeds going to charity.

Edward had high hopes: 'I would like the public to view it in a generous way – seeing that members of the Royal Family are, in reality, ordinary human beings. We're not superstars. And I hope, at the end of the competition, the Royal Family will come out of it much better.' But the programme was not exactly a success. The media had a field day and royal dignity was severely dented. Prince Philip commented to a BBC executive, 'Why doesn't Edward let the TV people get on with it and just turn up to accept the cheques? He's making us look foolish.'

How Normal is Normal?

'There's a lot of baggage that comes with us, trust me, a lot of baggage,' Prince William observed sagely. His brother added, 'Our friends have to put up with a lot when it comes to us.'

Harry admitted, 'There's a lot of times that both myself and my brother wish, obviously, that we were just completely normal.' And if he were 'normal'? 'I don't know how well this would get on, but I'd probably live in Africa ... as a job, it would probably be a safari guide ... within our private life and within certain other parts of our life we want to be as normal as possible ... It's hard, because to a certain respect we never will be normal.'

'You may be abnormal,' William retorted, 'I'm pretty normal … Deep down I am pretty normal.'

Shortly before leaving on a visit to the US, Prince Harry reflected, 'Every time I get to meet kids and they have been told a real-life prince is coming, the disappointment on their faces when they see me without a crown or a cape.'

The fascination with the latest generation continues and when the Duke and Duchess of Sussex launched their new Instagram account, @Sussexroyal, on 2 April 2019, it took just 5 hours and 45 minutes to attract a million followers, breaking the previous world record for speed. It now has over four million followers and counting.

Plucky Royals

As any celebrity who is constantly in the public eye will attest, fame can make you a target for cranks and worse. The Queen generally takes a robust approach to threats to her life, adopting a fatalistic attitude and acknowledging, 'If someone wants to get me, it is too easy.'

Princess Anne showed she was every bit her parents' daughter during a botched attempted kidnapping in March 1974. Ian

Ball, who had suffered from mental health problems, ambushed her car in the Mall and asked her to 'Come with me for a day or two' explaining, when she asked why, that he wanted £2 million. Anne famously retorted, 'Not bloody likely!' adding, 'And I haven't got £2 million', before she escaped from the car. Prime Minister Harold Wilson later commended Anne for her bravery. Ball had been armed and fired wildly into the car, wounding Anne's driver, bodyguard and a journalist who had come forward to help.

Afterwards, Anne admitted the attempted kidnap had made her much more wary: 'The difference now is that when I am on "walkabout" I think and act like a policeman – my eyes are everywhere.'

♔

Celebrating her official birthday on 13 June 1981, the Queen led the traditional Trooping the Colour parade as it set off from Buckingham Palace along the Mall towards Horse Guards Parade. Just before eleven o'clock, six shots were fired at the Queen from the crowd. Startled, her horse bolted forward, almost throwing her off. The unflappable Queen pulled on the reigns, entirely focused on calming and settling her horse. She then continued at a walking pace, smiling at the crowd, completing the ceremony.

Press and public were united in admiration of the Queen's resilience. The *Daily Express* summed it up: 'Her Majesty showed guts, courage, pluck, bravery and bottle.' In fact, the bullets turned out to have been blanks, fired by seventeen-year-old Marcus Sarjeant. He was quickly tackled and arrested by a collection of guardsmen, onlookers and police, and later sentenced to five years in prison for 'intent to alarm'.

The Queen afterwards admitted that in the instant before the shots rang out she had actually glimpsed the gunman aiming at her from the crowd, but couldn't quite believe what she was seeing. She also said of her horse, Burmese, 'It wasn't the shots that frightened her but the Cavalry!' On hearing the shots, two Cavalrymen had spurred their horses forward to ride by the Queen's side, which further unsettled it.

Not surprisingly, the Queen's security was reviewed and it was agreed that in future members of the Household Cavalry would flank the Monarch during the parade. When the first one took his place beside her the following year, the Queen joked, 'You know why you're here. You're the one to get shot, not me.'

In 1982, the Queen woke in the early hours of a July morning to find a strange man standing by her bed. He was Michael Fagan, barefoot and bleeding from where he'd cut his hand breaking in through a Buckingham Palace window. With impressive cool, the Queen chatted calmly before she managed to alert security, using the excuse of fetching Fagan a cigarette to get away.

When the police finally arrived, one stopped to straighten his tie upon seeing Her Majesty. 'Oh, come on!' chivvied the exasperated Queen. 'Get a bloody move on.' Her footman, Paul Whybrew, said he thought it was Michael Fagan rather than the Queen who looked in need of a stiff drink to calm his nerves.

Later, the Queen amused family and friends with the story, including a chambermaid's startled reaction – 'Bloody 'ell ma'am, what's 'e doin' 'ere?' – and a perfect impersonation of the girl's Yorkshire accent.

Unable to sleep one warm summer night, the Queen decided to go outside for a walk in Buckingham Palace gardens, her preferred remedy for insomnia. A zealous security guard saw someone moving in the shadows. 'Who's there?' he challenged, when a familiar figure stepped out into the light.

'Bloody hell, Your Majesty!' exclaimed the surprised guard. 'I nearly shot you.' He swiftly apologised for his language. The Queen was unruffled by language or loaded gun, quipping, 'That's quite all right. Next time I'll ring through beforehand, so you don't have to shoot me.'

Incognito

Although the Queen is one of the most instantly recognizable figures on the world stage, some manage not to know her. Once she was out walking close to her Balmoral estate in the Highlands of Scotland, dressed appropriately for the weather in a heavy tweed coat and headscarf. Accompanied by her former police protection officer, Richard Griffin, she was approached by some American tourists who asked if she lived in the area. The Queen simply said that she had a house nearby, at which point the group asked if she had ever met the Queen. 'No,' she replied before pointing at her protection officer, 'but he has.' The group left, none the wiser.

♛

Stopped by a fellow shopper in the village grocers in Sandringham, the Queen was told, 'You do look like the Queen.' Smiling in response, Her Majesty answered, 'How very reassuring.'

♛

The Queen drove herself to the Royal Windsor Horse Show in 1991. It was virtually next door to Windsor Castle and she was driving a non-descript, unmarked car. At the entry to the VIP car park, the security guard didn't realise who she was and said, 'Sorry, love, you can't come in here without a sticker.' Opening the car window and looking the guard square in the eye, the Queen replied, 'I think, if you check, I'll be allowed to come in.'

While Prince Charles was in the Navy, he was approached by a group of press photographers hoping to take pictures of the young royal on duty. They failed to recognize the unshaven, rather scruffy officer who helpfully told them, 'Prince Charles? Oh, he won't see you. He's a pretty nasty piece of work, you know.'

On board the cruise liner *Queen Elizabeth*, an American fellow passenger was sure he knew the Queen Mother. She waited patiently for the penny to drop but instead he came up with, 'You advertise something – what is it?' The Queen Mother smiled modestly, 'Oh, it would be too unprofessional to tell you.'

Being constantly in the public eye must be wearing, and there are no doubt countless moments when Prince Philip would like to pass unnoticed. However, arriving late to give a speech at Cambridge University in 1997 was not one of them. 'Don't you know who I am? You bloody silly fool!' he snapped at a hapless car park attendant who had not recognized the royal driver.

The security guards who challenged Prince Andrew in September 2013 were also given a royal roasting. Andrew was taking an afternoon stroll through the Palace gardens when two armed police officers challenged him to 'verify your identity'. Andrew was outraged. 'Don't you know who I am?' he shouted angrily. The police officers later apologised personally and a few days after the incident, Andrew issued a statement saying, 'I am grateful for their apology and look forward to a safe walk in the garden in the future.'

Ma'am

When first meeting the Queen, protocol dictates that she should be addressed as 'Your Majesty', after which it is 'Ma'am' to rhyme with 'jam' until she is leaving when it is back to 'Your Majesty'. The same goes for other female members of the Royal Family with 'Your Royal Highness' in place of 'Your Majesty'.

When photographer Norman Parkinson was photographing the three Windsor women, the Queen, Queen Mother and Princess Margaret together in 1980, all dressed in identical deep-blue satin capes, he had not foreseen the difficulties. His usual directions, 'Turn to the right, ma'am', or 'Chin up a little, ma'am', simply led to confusion.

'It's absolutely no use you "ma'aming" us like this,' Margaret explained. 'We haven't the slightest idea who you are referring to. We are all ma'am.' The resulting photograph hangs in the National Portrait Gallery in London.

CHAPTER 6

In the Saddle

With their busy day-to-day lives, you could be forgiven for assuming the Royal Family would like to take it easy during their leisure time. In fact, they prefer being active, playing sports and keeping fit. The whole family love horses and riding, and the Queen has also made something of an alternative career breeding racehorses.

Her horses have won all the Classic British races, with the exception of the Epsom Derby, though she hasn't given up trying and had high hopes for her horse Sextant in 2019. She famously reads the racing newspaper *Racing Post* most mornings, and in 2017 alone earned almost £400,000 in prize money.

Prince Philip would generally rather take part in sport than watch, enjoying being active and competitive. 'Everything you do is based on competition unless some half-witted teacher seems to think it's bad for you. People like to pit their abilities against someone else. People want to race each other. It's what gives the whole thing spice.'

Arriving at Westminster Abbey for her coronation on 2 June 1953, one of the Queen's attendants commented, 'You must be feeling nervous, ma'am.' The Abbey was packed with sovereigns from around the world, heads of state and other dignitaries. The lengthy ceremony was being televised for the first time and an estimated 27 million people were watching in the UK, with millions more worldwide.

'Of course I am,' the Queen replied. 'But I really do think Aureole will win.' She was talking about her horse due to run in the Derby four days later. In the end he was the runner-up, second to Pinza.

The Queen's sheer enjoyment and excitement at the races is obvious, and never more so than when one of her horses is winning. Her exhilaration was caught on film when Free Agent became her twentieth winner at the Chesham Stakes in 2008. The two-year-old colt broke through almost at the last moment and won conclusively. Much to everyone's surprise, the Queen sprang to her feet and punched the air triumphantly shouting, 'I've done it!' Her racing manager, John Warren, struggled to keep up with the Monarch as she dashed off to greet her horse. 'It was a moment of real joy … she raced to the paddock like she was twenty,' he commented.

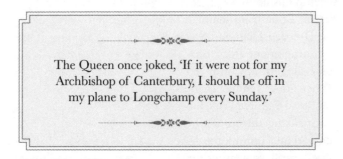

The Queen once joked, 'If it were not for my Archbishop of Canterbury, I should be off in my plane to Longchamp every Sunday.'

The Queen Mother was an avid racing fan, a patron of National Hunt racing while the Queen has always preferred the flat. During their daily phone calls, conversation would invariably turn to horses and all things related. Writing to her mother from New Zealand, the Queen observed, 'Racing is incredible out here. They all bet like mad and like their marathons of eight races at a dose.'

Charles shared his grandmother's appreciation of National Hunt steeplechasing, explaining, 'It's a great challenge to try to overcome a certain element of natural fear … going flatout over fences and wondering if you are going to get to the other side in one piece.' Like his mother he finds time out on horseback offers a sense of freedom that is a wonderful antidote to the stresses of day-to-day life. 'If I didn't get the exercise – or have something to take my mind off things – I would go potty.'

Princess Anne inherited her mother's love of horses and is an accomplished horsewoman. She was European cross-country champion in 1971 and won silver medals in the European Championship in 1975, both individually and as part of the British Equestrian team. In 1987, when she was riding in the Dresden Diamond Stakes at Ascot, the Queen shouted encouragement from the stands: 'Don't be so cool – do something!' It obviously did the trick as Anne went on to win on her horse Ten No Trumps, becoming the first member of the Royal Family to ride an Ascot winner.

Speaking during her years of competitive riding, Anne said, 'When I'm approaching a water jump, with dozens of photographers waiting for me to fall in, and hundreds of spectators wondering what's going to happen next, the horse is just about the only one who doesn't know I am royal.'

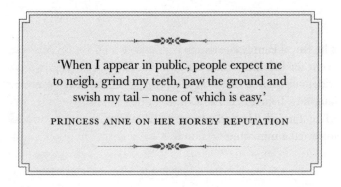

'When I appear in public, people expect me to neigh, grind my teeth, paw the ground and swish my tail – none of which is easy.'

PRINCESS ANNE ON HER HORSEY REPUTATION

Anne explained her decision to give up competing: 'There's a moment in sport when the enjoyment wears off because of the pressure put on you to be successful. That is the moment to stop and make sure in your own mind what sport is all about.' But she still takes an active interest in equestrian events and couldn't help commenting wryly, 'In my day, you were the person to blame, not the horse.'

In May 2007, the Queen realized a long-held wish to attend the Kentucky Derby. She and Philip stayed with old friends at their ranch. Relaxing in the early evening sunshine, she had been following her granddaughter Zara Phillip's progress at the Badminton Horse trials, and couldn't help fretting about her performance complaining, 'Nobody pays any attention to what Granny thinks!'

Having represented Britain herself in the 1976 Montreal Olympics, Princess Anne was very much the proud mother awarding daughter Zara a silver medal at the equestrian events in Greenwich Park during the 2012 London Olympics. Maybe she listened to Granny's advice.

The Royal Family clearly enjoy themselves at Ascot. This is an event for fun more than business. In June 2019, photos were widely circulated of the Queen and her granddaughter Zara laughing heartily at Zara's husband, England rugby player Mike Tindall. He had whipped off his top hat with a flourish to reveal a miniature version hidden underneath.

Prince William's nursery school teacher was somewhat taken aback when the four-year-old announced, 'Whisky is such fun!' He was talking about his first pony called Whisky.

In 1965, Prince Philip ('I'm not really a talented spectator, frankly … I'd rather do something') famously claimed, 'The only active sport I follow is polo, and most of the work is done by the pony.' That, however, hides his competitive nature. When visiting Pakistan, he passed up the opportunity to play polo, afterwards explaining, 'I went … on serious business. If I'd gone there to play polo I'd have got in some practice beforehand.'

Prince Philip eventually gave up polo in 1971, taking up carriage driving a couple of years later because it was, he thought, 'the perfect sport for middle age'. It also seemed the logical choice. 'I gave up polo when I turned fifty and then this started and I thought, "Well, you've got horses and carriages, why don't you have a go?"' He claimed somewhat implausibly, given his active nature, that 'I took it up as a geriatric sport. I thought of it as a retirement exercise. I promise you, when I set out I thought it would be a nice weekend activity, rather like a golfing weekend. Which it was until some idiot asked me to be a member of the British team.'

After hitting a tree and overturning his carriage in a 1974 race, Philip was not in the best humour when a journalist asked if he enjoyed the sport. 'Don't be a fool,' he snapped. 'Do you think I do it for penance?' And, when asked if carriage driving got in the way of his royal duties, he replied, 'It's the other way around. The duties get in the way of the driving.'

Philip was President of the International Equestrian Federation and responsible for drawing up the rules for competitive carriage driving. To a Chinese official's query about protocol, he was disarmingly casual: 'As far as we are concerned, you can play "Colonel Bogey" and fly a pair of knickers from the flagpole as your team enters the arena.'

Although the 97-year-old Philip no longer competes, he still enjoys driving a carriage. Waiting for the arrival of Harry and Meghan's first child in May 2019, he took his horses out for a gallop around Home Park at Windsor, his only concessions to age being to take his groom along and wrapping up against the elements.

When Prince Charles was learning to play polo as a teenager, his father apparently told his coaches, 'Let him have it hot and strong. Be frank and fearless.'

The tough approach obviously didn't put Charles off: 'I feel a hundred times better after a game of polo.' It did, however, encourage his competitive side, particularly with his father and, after he learned to ski, he was quick to tell Philip, who had never really taken to the slopes, 'I've got one sport you haven't now.'

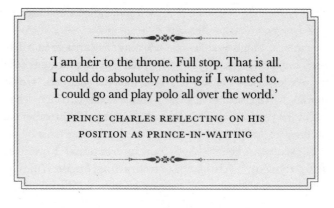

'I am heir to the throne. Full stop. That is all.
I could do absolutely nothing if I wanted to.
I could go and play polo all over the world.'

PRINCE CHARLES REFLECTING ON HIS
POSITION AS PRINCE-IN-WAITING

Prince Philip is a well-known cricket fan who has been known to hide a radio in his top hat when attending Ascot in order to follow the day's events. The Queen also enjoys it and appears to take the England team's performance personally. The story goes that a new member of staff at Balmoral was more than a little surprised to come upon the Monarch jumping up and down with glee, exclaiming, 'I've won, I've won!' She had just heard that England's test team had defeated the Australians.

Any book on Prince Philip's quotes needs a section on cricket. His many comments on the sport include …

'The last time I played in a village match I was given LBW first ball. That is the sort of umpiring that should be looked into.'

When Brian Johnston interviewed Philip on BBC radio's *Test Match Special*, he asked how modern cricket could be improved. Philip quipped, 'I only wish to God that some of their trousers fitted better.'

After opening a new stand at Lord's – in one of his last-ever public engagements in May 2017, just a few months before his retirement – Philip was shown a selection of historic cricket bats including a huge, baseball-style bat with an extra-long handle that is now ruled illegal. He joked to former England cricket captain, Mike Gatting, 'It's an offensive weapon.'

And, on a visit to Lord's Cricket Ground in 2009, Philip was asked by an MCC official whether he had enjoyed his lunch. 'Why do you ask that?' 'I hoped the answer would be yes,' the official replied. 'What a stupid question,' the Prince retorted.

♛

Announcing the launch of the Invictus Games, a new multi-sport championship for injured servicemen and women, in March 2014, Prince Harry explained, 'I suppose it is one time when you can really use your name to raise money. And if I am going to use it for anything, what more of a better opportunity [than] to use it here.' Furthermore, 'I have witnessed first-hand how the power of sport can positively impact the lives of wounded, injured and sick servicemen and women in their journey of recovery. The Invictus Games will focus on what they can achieve post-injury and celebrate their fighting spirit, through an inclusive sporting competition that recognizes the sacrifice they have made.'

Not All Sports Are Equal

Prince William has a permanent reminder of why he should be wary of golf. As an eight-year-old he had an operation at Great Ormond Street children's hospital in London after fracturing his skull. He had been playing with friends on the putting green at Ludgrove School when the accident happened. 'My Harry Potter scar, as I call it, just here [pointing at his forehead]. I call it that because it glows sometimes and some people notice it – other times they don't notice it at all. I got hit by a golf club when I was playing golf with a friend of mine. Yeah, we were on a putting green and the next thing you know there was a seven-iron and it came out of nowhere and it hit me in the head.'

When asked to give a speech at a golfing dinner in 1949, Philip opened with, 'Prepare for a shock. I do not play golf.' And Anne – 'Golf seems to be an arduous way to go for a walk. I prefer to take the dogs out.'

Perhaps mindful of his golfing scar, Prince William confessed, 'I gave up playing hockey when a friend of mine had his teeth knocked out. Put me off a bit.'

Princess Anne is not a fan, either. 'I gave up hockey as soon as possible and I didn't like netball because I used to get wolf whistles in my short skirt. I was a bit of a softie and I didn't like rough games.'

The Queen attends a range of sporting fixtures as part of her official duties, and has often presented the winning trophies. She used to present the cup to the winners of the FA Cup final, but handed this task over to William when he became President of the FA in May 2006, in place of his uncle, Andrew.

'Football's a difficult business and aren't they prima donnas? But it's a wonderful game,' the Queen commented while knighting the FA Premier League chairman, David Richards, in November 2006.

Launching Heads Up in 2019, Prince William explained that the initiative, in collaboration with the Football Association, aimed to use football as a way of starting 'the biggest ever conversation on mental health'.

Football and mental health are both issues close to William's heart. 'We can spend hours in the pub talking about the injuries holding back our club's top players … We wouldn't think twice to ask a mate how he was doing after he broke an arm or an ankle,' he continued. 'We wouldn't hesitate to talk about our routine at the gym, or even our need to make it a bit more regular. But when it comes to our mental health, we – and, by we, I mean men in particular – often have nothing to say at all.'

CHAPTER 7

Candid Comments: the Palace, the Press and the Public

P rince Philip has a reputation for not holding back when it comes to voicing his opinions. Look more closely and the Royal Family as a whole has been remarkably candid in expressing exactly how they feel on occasion, even the Queen, who is remarkably tight-lipped and rarely blunders: 'My father told me that whatever I said or did, to anyone, they would remember it.' Her unofficial doctrine is apparently, 'never complain, never explain'.

However, if there's one subject that unites members of the Royal Family across the generations, it's their feelings about the press. Over the years, their interactions with the media have tended to bring out the wickedest side of the royal wit.

When Edward took a job as a production assistant for Andrew Lloyd Webber's Really Useful Theatre Company in 1988, the press was full of reports that he would be a 'real dogsbody' with a range of duties including making the tea. Greeted by a bank of reporters on his first day asking if he was looking forward to his new role, the Prince joked, 'Of course. Look at me, I've got my tea bags ready.'

Edward also commented, 'There's a difference between a public function when you know the press will be there and a private one where, to me, their presence is an invasion of privacy. I don't mind a photograph being taken on the lawn.'

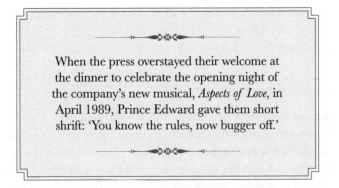

When the press overstayed their welcome at
the dinner to celebrate the opening night of
the company's new musical, *Aspects of Love*, in
April 1989, Prince Edward gave them short
shrift: 'You know the rules, now bugger off.'

Princess Anne has been one of the harshest critics of the press,
stating her position clearly: 'I stand somewhere to the right of
Genghis Khan in my attitude to the press. Alfred the Great in
the ninth century took a stronger line. Persistent slanderers had
their tongues cut out.' She also reasoned, 'If the press can be so
wrong, so trivial and so irresponsible about the Royal Family,
the subject I know most about, then they may be wrong, trivial,
irresponsible, etc., about everything else.'

When asked to pose for a photograph, Princess
Anne refused point blank: 'I don't do stunts.'
And she was characteristically blunt when
she pointed out, 'You are a pest, by the very
nature of that camera in your hand.'

But, praise where praise is due. Anne was pragmatic about
the change in the media's portrayal of her as a 'good thing'

after her 1982 Save the Children Fund tour through eight countries in Africa, commenting, 'I did notice my miraculous transformation ... It's nice when one reads something pleasant.'

During the height of the press's obsession with Diana, the Queen complained to a journalist, 'My daughter-in-law can't even go into a shop to buy wine gums because of you.' His flip response – 'Can't she send a servant to buy them?' – left Her Majesty completely unimpressed and led to a politely withering put down: 'That, if you don't mind me saying so, is an extremely pompous remark to make.'

And, of course, Diana and the press is a Big Subject. During her second pregnancy she said, 'I had a very bad time with the press – they literally haunted and hunted me. I haven't felt well since day one. I don't think I'm made for the production line.' On another occasion she observed, 'I made the grave mistake once of saying to a child I was thick as a plank, in order to ease the child's nervousness, which it did. But that headline went all round the world, and I rather regret saying it.'

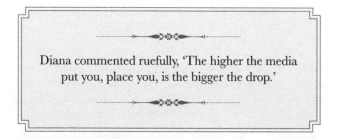

Diana commented ruefully, 'The higher the media put you, place you, is the bigger the drop.'

Diana came to accept that there was no getting away from media attention: 'They've decided that I'm still a product after fifteen, sixteen years, that sells well, and they all shout at me, telling me that: "Oh, come on, Di, look up. If you give us a picture I can get my children to a better school."' No wonder she once said, 'I simply treat the press as though they were children.'

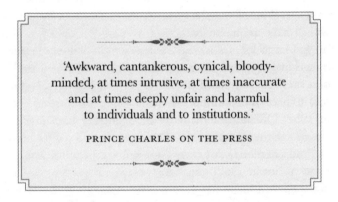

Charles has alluded to his misrepresentation in the press and obviously feels misunderstood. During one official engagement he turned to journalists and asked, 'Have any of you the slightest idea what I'm doing here?'

'Awkward, cantankerous, cynical, bloody-minded, at times intrusive, at times inaccurate and at times deeply unfair and harmful to individuals and to institutions.'

PRINCE CHARLES ON THE PRESS

Taking a more measured view of the media, he once stated, 'As I get older, I find less privacy becomes available and more people seem to be interested in every small and minute aspect of one's life. Somehow you have to have the outlook or philosophy which enables you to bear it, otherwise, I promise you, it's very easy to go mad.'

In addition, 'I look at it from a newspaperman's point of view: he's got a job to do – I've got a job to do. At times they happen to coincide, and compromise must occur, otherwise misery can so easily ensue. I try to put myself in their shoes, and

I hope they try to put themselves in mine, although I appreciate that is difficult.'

Joking about the press, Charles noted, 'It's when nobody wants to write about you or take photographs of you that you ought to worry in my sort of job.' On the other hand, the press are 'bloody people', and he ordered one particularly persistent photographer to 'Get out of the way, you annoying little prat.'

Don't get Prince Philip started about the press. Beginning gently with 'I have frequently been misrepresented. I don't hate the press; I find a lot of it is very unpalatable.' The Prince became increasingly cynical. He was infuriated by media speculation of a rift between himself and the Queen during his six-month solo tour of the Commonwealth during the winter of 1956 to 1957. Official statements to the contrary only served to encourage the gossip.

And, after the *Daily Express* had published a series of revealing royal stories in 1962, he complained it was 'a bloody awful newspaper ... full of lies, scandal and imagination ... a vicious newspaper.' To the matron of a Caribbean hospital during a visit in 1968, 'Well, you have mosquitoes, we have the press.'

In the 1990s, he commented despairingly, 'Day after day there was a derogatory story about one member of the family or another'. And, in 1996, he told President Jacques Chirac of France, 'If we had your laws, the British press could not have done so much damage to the Royal Family.' Three years later, he complained that 'the press have turned us into a soap opera'.

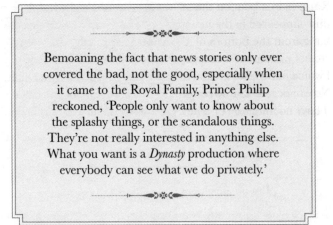

Bemoaning the fact that news stories only ever
covered the bad, not the good, especially when
it came to the Royal Family, Prince Philip
reckoned, 'People only want to know about
the splashy things, or the scandalous things.
They're not really interested in anything else.
What you want is a *Dynasty* production where
everybody can see what we do privately.'

In 2006, Prince Philip told Jeremy Paxman, 'I don't read the
tabloids … I glance at one [broadsheet]. I reckon one's enough.
I can't cope with them. But the Queen reads every bloody paper
she can lay her hands on.' This wasn't always the case. In the
early days of the Queen's reign Philip would regularly check
all the papers at breakfast saying, 'Let's see what I'm supposed
to have done wrong yesterday.'

Philip reserves a particular level of vitriol for NewsCorp
owner Rupert Murdoch. In 2006, his comment on the media
mogul was damning, 'His anti-establishment views really pulled
the plug on an awful lot of things that we hold to be quite
reasonable and sensible institutions.'

Princess Margaret had no affection for the media, claiming,
'I have been misreported and misrepresented since the age
of seventeen.' She recalled the first time a fabricated story
appeared in the press; she had been with some of her fellow Sea

Rangers in a boat on the lake at Frogmore. 'And what do you think appeared in the newspapers? They said I had pulled the bung from the bottom of the boat! That made me frightfully cross. I was part of a team and very proud of it, I might tell you. I would never have dreamt of doing something so irresponsible.' No wonder she saw no reason to justify or explain herself, stating, 'I have no intention of telling people what I have for breakfast.'

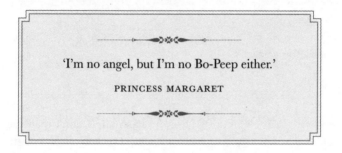

'I'm no angel, but I'm no Bo-Peep either.'

PRINCESS MARGARET

And Margaret on the Queen – 'It was inevitable, when there are two sisters and one is the Queen … [she] … must be the source of honour and all that is good, while the other must be the focus of the most creative malice, the evil sister.'

Kate, Duchess of Cambridge, has tried to adopt a philosophical attitude to what is written about her: 'You sort of have to ignore a lot of what's said, obviously take it on board, but you have to be yourself really.'

On the same subject, Sarah, Duchess of York, admitted, 'I, on the other hand, completely believed every single thing they wrote. I believed I was the worthless person they were talking about.' When revelatory stories of her were appearing regularly, she found it hard not to take everything personally, 'I was devastated to pick up a newspaper the other day and read that 82 per cent of British men would rather sleep with a goat than with me.'

Prince William said bluntly, 'I don't need the press to tell me what to do.' While his brother commented, 'It is the media that stamp an image on me that really isn't me.' Although known to be extremely wary of the press, Harry joked to reporters as he turned his back and began digging to plant a tree, 'You've got the best view!'

Ask a Stupid Question

Prince Philip is never one to suffer fools gladly and nothing prompts his sarcasm more than an obvious question. Leaving hospital after treatment for an infection following the Queen's

'Damn fool question!' the Prince snapped at journalist Caroline Wyatt at a banquet at the Elysee Palace in 2006. She had dared to ask the Queen if she was enjoying her visit to Paris. And when asked by a journalist if he would care to give his opinion of the new British Embassy in Berlin, opened by the Queen in 2000, Philip was brief and to the point, 'No'.

Diamond Jubilee celebrations, he was asked if he was feeling better, 'Well, I wouldn't be coming out if I wasn't,' he snapped. And in 2005, when a reporter made the mistake of asking, 'I wonder if you might like to talk to me?' he replied briskly, 'Well, you can carry on wondering.'

Members of the public are not exempt from his sarcasm. Touching down in Canada after a long flight, Philip was asked by a local VIP, 'What was your flight like Your Royal Highness?' 'Have you ever flown in a plane?' he replied, a cold glint in his eyes. 'Oh, yes, sir, many times,' the eager official answered. 'Well,' said Prince Philip, moving in for the kill, 'it was just like that.'

Sounding more than a little like her father, when a reporter commented that it was lovely to see her again, Princess Anne asked drily, 'Oh, really? Why?'

Who Are You?

Over the years, the Queen has occasionally failed to recognize well-known celebs. The royal information feed was obviously not working when she met guitar legend Eric Clapton at a Buckingham Palace reception in 2005. She asked politely, 'Have you been playing a long time?' He replied without a trace of irony, 'It must be forty-five years now.' When introduced to renowned Brit artist Tracey Emin at the newly opened Turner Contemporary Art Centre in Kent, in 2011, the Sovereign enquired, 'Do you show internationally as well as in Margate?' And when meeting historian Andrew Roberts, who was giving Kate a lesson on the history of the monarchy just before her wedding to Prince William, the Queen was firmly convinced he was one of the Palace butlers.

The Queen Mother remembered, 'We had this rather lugubrious man in a suit and he read a poem … I think it was called "The Desert" … At first the girls got the giggles, then I did, then even the King.' The poet? T. S. Eliot and he had been reading 'The Waste Land', one of the most renowned and quoted poems of the twentieth century.

On meeting Sir Michael Bishop, who was chairman of Channel 4 at the time, Prince Philip was clearly not impressed: 'So you're responsible for the kind of crap Channel 4 produces!' And at a Buckingham Palace reception in 2000, he spotted a group of female Labour MPs who were all wearing name badges bearing the title 'Ms'. 'Ah,' said the Prince, 'so this is feminist corner then.' No wonder, then, that in a 1960 speech to the General Dental Council he added, 'Dontopedalogy is the science of opening your mouth and putting your foot in it, a science which I have practised for a good many years.'

True to form, when Philip noticed well-known republican editor-in-chief of *The Independent* Simon Kelner at a Windsor Castle press reception, celebrating the Golden Jubilee in 2002, he asked him what he thought he was doing there. On being told that Philip had himself sent the invitation, the Prince retorted, 'Well, you didn't have to come!'

Got Any Earplugs?

No one, not even celebs, can avoid a Prince Philip put-down. He attended his first Royal Variety Performance with the Queen in 1952 and has sat through rather a lot of the shows since then. It is a tradition that the royals meet the performers backstage after the show. Hence, a 1969 photo showing Prince Philip and Tom Jones laughing together, apparently sharing a joke. Not so. 'What do you gargle with – pebbles?' Philip asked. The next day Philip added, 'It is very difficult at all to see how it is possible to become immensely valuable by singing what I think are the most hideous songs.' A few months later at a small-business lunch discussing how hard it was to make a fortune in Britain, Philip returned to the topic: 'What about Tom Jones? He's made a million and he's a bloody awful singer.' And as for Elton John … When he began to sing at the 2001 Royal Variety Performance, the Queen said to Philip, 'I wish he'd turn his microphone to the side.' He had a better suggestion, 'I wish he'd turn his microphone off.'

In 2002, Prince Philip asked, 'Are we going to need earplugs?' He had just been told that Madonna would be singing the *Die Another Day* Bond theme.

This was not the only time that year that Philip insulted Elton: The singer-songwriter, is a near neighbour of the royal couple as he also owns a house in Windsor. Hearing that Elton had sold his Watford Football club-themed Aston Martin, Philip exclaimed, 'Oh, it's you that owns that ghastly car, is it? We often see it when driving to Windsor Castle.'

Prince Philip isn't the only one with strong views on celebs. In 1960, the Everly Brothers performed their hit song 'Cathy's Clown'. This time it was the Queen who was unimpressed, commenting, 'They sound like two cats being strangled.' And aiming to put Sharon Osborne at ease after the television personality had sworn while attempting to compliment Camilla, the Duchess reassured her, 'It's quite all right, we curse quite a lot around here.'

More Royal Gaffes

The Queen is usually the model of diplomacy but there have been a few lapses over the years. On a proposed visit to the northern city, she remarked, 'Manchester, that's not such a nice place.' And regarding Niagara Falls on a tour of Canada, she sounded less than impressed when she observed, 'It looks very damp.'

Before visiting Kingston-upon-Hull in 1957, the Queen amended a speech on the grounds that she was happy to say 'I am pleased to be in Kingston today,' but would not say, 'I am very pleased …' The town had recently been described as one of the 'few dogged bastions of republicanism' in the country by *The Times*.

> The Queen uses the phrase 'How fascinating'
> or 'How interesting' to mean a variety of
> different things, and often to show she disagrees
> with an opinion. It's all in the tone and can
> be witheringly effective. Known to dislike
> pomposity and anyone taking themselves too
> seriously, off the record Her Majesty described
> one 'self-made toff' as a 'ghastly little crawler'.

Prince Philip's gaffes, or 'Philipisms', have inspired a number of books and websites. He remains largely unrepentant, and is adamant that 'I rather doubt whether anyone has ever been genuinely shocked by anything I have said.'

He likes to make people laugh and put them at ease. At the age of twenty-one, Philip wrote to a relative, 'I am rude but it is fun.' When it was announced that he was retiring at the age of ninety-six, he joked, 'Standing down? I can barely stand up.'

Most people, even those who are on the receiving end of one of his jokes, find him charming and, with a deft word, he can defuse the tension from even the most formal of royal occasions. Interviewed in 1999, Philip said, 'I don't think I have ever got up to make a speech … and not made the audience laugh at least once.'

And now for what you've been waiting for …

Visiting the Samuel Whitbread Community College in Bedfordshire, Philip looked in on a science class. 'Is there any sign of intelligent life in this classroom?' he asked. Surprised teacher Wendy Hill stuttered, 'I wouldn't know.' 'Well, you should know!' reprimanded Philip. The teacher later said she considered it 'a privilege to have been so soundly ticked off by Prince Philip. It made my day.'

On a visit to China in 1986, he pronounced Beijing 'Ghastly!' He delivered the same verdict about Stoke-on-Trent to the city's MP, Joan Walley, at Buckingham Palace in 1997.

Having a bad day in Canada in 1976, Philip snapped grumpily, 'We don't come here for our health. We can think of other ways of enjoying ourselves.'

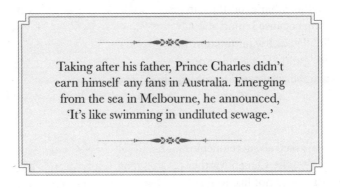

Taking after his father, Prince Charles didn't earn himself any fans in Australia. Emerging from the sea in Melbourne, he announced, 'It's like swimming in undiluted sewage.'

When visiting the Cayman Islands in 1994, Philip enquired, 'Aren't most of you descended from pirates?'

And he asked a rather surprised British student who was trekking in Papua New Guinea in 1998, 'You managed not to get eaten, then?'

Speaking totally out of turn in Scotland, in August 1999, Philip's verdict on an old-fashioned fuse box was, 'It looks as though it was put in by an Indian.' But this was too big a faux pas even for Philip to laugh off, and he later tried to correct his comment. 'I meant to say cowboy. I just got my cowboys and Indians mixed up.'

Let Us Not Take Ourselves Too Seriously

With so many photos of himself to choose from, Prince Charles is under no illusions, 'I've got a long body and short legs. And please don't blame photographers for making my ears look large. They are large.' And feeling cheerful as he left hospital after a hernia operation, Charles joked, 'Hernia today, gone tomorrow.'

Other Charles off-the-cuff remarks include: 'I'm a dangerous person because I mind about things'; 'Sometimes I'm a bit of a twit'; 'What I want to know is: what is actually wrong with an elite?'; and 'The whole imposing edifice of modern medicine is like the celebrated tower of Pisa – slightly off balance.'

When asked about retouching a photograph to airbrush out her wrinkles, the Queen Mother preferred it left true to life, after all, 'I would not like to feel I had lived all these years without having anything to show for it.'

Looking at the first official double portrait of himself and his brother, painted by Nicky Philipps in 2009, Prince Harry was unsure: 'I don't know, I'm a little bit more ginger in there than I am in real life, I think. I don't know, and William got given more hair so, apart from that, it is what it is. But no, it's nice. It could have been worse.'

He also said, 'The most amusing point is meeting somebody and them going, "You're so not what I thought you were." And well, 'what did you think? "Oh, best not to say it to your face." Well, thanks a lot!'

Princess Diana joked, 'They say it is better to be poor and happy than rich and miserable, but how about a compromise, like moderately rich and just moody?'

The evening after Prince Charles and Diana's wedding on 29 July 1981, the Queen's cousin Lady Elizabeth Anson hosted a party at Claridge's for five hundred guests, including the Queen and Prince Philip. Television screens played video highlights from the elaborate wedding ceremony at St Paul's Cathedral. Relaxed, watching the footage while sipping a dry martini, the Queen suddenly exclaimed, 'Oh, Philip, do look! I'm wearing my Miss Piggy face.'

When Camilla broke her leg and strained a shoulder ligament at the same time, she laughed at herself, 'I've got no leg and an arm on one side, and no arm and a leg on the other.'

When the Royal Family go anywhere, they tend to be met by the smell of fresh paint and red carpets. Prince Charles mused, 'I sometimes wonder if two-thirds of the globe is covered in red carpet.' The no-nonsense Prince thought, 'The man who invented the red carpet needed his head examined.'

Bibliography

Arscott, David, *Queen Elizabeth II Diamond Jubilee 60 Years a Queen: A Very Peculiar History*, Book House, 2012

Bedell Smith, Sally, *Elizabeth The Queen*, Penguin Random House, 2012

Botham, Noel and Montague, Bruce, *The Book of Royal Useless Information*, John Blake Publishing, 2012

Bradford, Sarah, *Elizabeth: A Biography of Her Majesty the Queen*, Booksales, 2002

Brandreth, Gyles, *Philip and Elizabeth: Portrait of a Marriage*, Arrow Books, 2004

Butt, Antony A., *The Wisdom of Prince Philip*, Hardie Grant Books, 2015

Burrell, Paul, *A Royal Duty*, Penguin 2004

Carey, George, *Know the Truth: A Memoir*, HarperCollins, 2004

Cawthorne, Nigel, *I Know I am Rude But it is Fun: Prince Philip on Prince Philip*, Gibson Square, 2016

Clarke, Stephen, *Elizabeth II, Queen of Laughs*, Stephen Clarke, 2018

Crosland, Susan, *Tony Crosland*, Jonathan Cape, 1982

Crossman, Richard, ed. Anthony Howard, *The Crossman Diaries*, Hamish Hamilton/Jonathan Cape, 1976

Dampier, Phil and Walton, Ashley, *Prince Philip: Wise Words and Golden Gaffes*, Barzipan Publishing, 2012

Dampier, Phil and Walton, Ashley, *What's in the Queen's Handbag and Other Royal Secrets*, Book Guild Publishing, 2007

Dolby, Karen, *The Wicked Wit of Prince Philip*, Michael O'Mara Books, 2017

Dolby, Karen, *The Wicked Wit of Princess Margaret*, Michael O'Mara Books, 2018

Dolby, Karen, *The Wicked Wit of Queen Elizabeth II*, Michael O'Mara Books, 2015

Eade, Philip, *Young Prince Philip: His Turbulent Early Life*, HarperPress, 2011

Hardman, Robert, *Monarchy: The Royal Family at Work*, Ebury, 2007

Hardman, Robert, *Queen of the World*, Century, 2018

Heald, Tim, *The Duke: A Portrait of Prince Philip*, Hodder & Stoughton, 1991

Hennessy, Peter, *Having it So Good*, Allen Lane, 2006

Hoey, Brian, *At Home with The Queen*, HarperCollins, 2002

Hoey, Brian, *Not in Front of the Corgis*, The Robson Press, 2011

Johnstone-Bryden, Richard, *The Royal Yacht* Britannia: *The Official History*, Conway Maritime Press, 2003

Junor, Penny, *The Duchess: The Untold Story*, William Collins, 2017

Junor, Penny, *The Firm*, HarperCollins, 2011

Lacey, Robert, *Royal: Her Majesty Queen Elizabeth II*, Little Brown, 2002

Leibovitz, Annie, *At Work*, Phaidon Press, 2018

Longford, Elizabeth, *Elizabeth R*, Weidenfeld & Nicolson, 1983

Marr, Andrew, *Diamond Queen: Elizabeth II and Her People*, Macmillan UK, 2011

Moody, Marcia, *Kate: A Biography*, Michael O'Mara Books, 2013

Muscat, Julian, *Her Majesty's Pleasure*, Racing Post Books, 2012

Nicholl, Katie, *Harry: Life, Loss, and Love*, Hachette Books, 2018

Nicholl, Katie, *Kate: The Future Queen*, Hachette Books, 2013

Nicholl, Katie, *William and Harry*, Preface Publishing, 2010

Obama, Michelle, *Becoming*, Viking, 2018

Parker, Michael, *It's All Going Terribly Wrong*, Benefactum Publishing, 2013

Petrella, Kate, *Royal Wisdom: The Most Daft, Cheeky, and Brilliant Quotes from Britain's Royal Family*, Adams Media, 2011

Pimlott, Ben, *The Queen: Elizabeth II and the Monarchy*, HarperPress, 2012

Prince Philip, *Men, Machines & Sacred Cows*, Hamish Hamilton, 1984

Prince Philip, *Prince Philip Speaks: Selected Speeches 1956–1959*, Collins Clear-Type Press, 1960

Prince Philip, *Selected Speeches, 1948–1955*, Oxford University Press, 1957

Rhodes, Margaret, *The Final Curtsey*, Birlinn Ltd and Umbria Press, 2012

Scarfe, Rory, *Do You Still Throw Spears at Each Other? 90 Years of Glorious Gaffes from the Duke*, Simon & Schuster, 2011

Seward, Ingrid, *My Husband and I: The Inside Story of 70 Years of the Royal Marriage*, Simon and Schuster, 2017

Sinclair, Marianne and Litvinoff, Sarah, ed., *The Wit and Wisdom of the Royal Family*, Plexus Publishing, 1990

Websites

www.albertjack.com
www.allgreatquotes.com
www.apnews.com
www.azquotes.com
www.bbc.co.uk
www.biography.com
www.brainyquote.com
www.britroyals.com
www.cheatsheet.com
www.dailymail.co.uk

www.dianaslegacy.co.uk
www.express.co.uk
www.facebook.com/
    TheBritishMonarchy
www.famousquotesand
    authors.com
www.gq-magazine.co.uk
www.graziadaily.co.uk
www.guardian.co.uk
www.harpersbazaar.com

www.hellomagazine.com
www.historicnewspapers.
  co.uk
www.historyextra.com
www.huffingtonpost.com
www.imdb.com
www.independent.co.uk
www.inews.co.uk
www.itv.com
www.majestymagazine.co.uk
www.marieclaire.co.uk
www.military.com
www.mirror.co.uk
www.news.sky.com
www.nowtolove.co.nz
www.nytimes.com
www.radiotimes.com
uk.reuters.com
www.royal.uk
www.royal.gov.uk

www.saidwhat.co.uk
www.scotsman.com
www.sky.com
www.telegraph.co.uk
www.thesun.co.uk
www.thetimes.co.uk
www.thinkexist.com
www.time.com
www.timesonline.co.uk
www.trueroyalty.tv
www.upi.com
www.yorkshireeveningpost.
  co.uk
www.yorkshirepost.co.uk
www.vanityfair.com
www.vice.com
www.vox.com
www.youtube.com
en.wikipedia.org

Picture credits

Page 9: Keystone-France / Gamma-Rapho via Getty Images.
Page 31: Keystone Press / Alamy.
Page 61: Tim Graham Photo Library via Getty Images.
Page 77: Karwai Tang / WireImage / Getty Images.
Page 97: Tim Graham Photo Library via Getty Images.
Page 127: Bride Lane Library / Popperfoto via Getty Images.
Page 139: Tim Graham Photo Library via Getty Images.